the monster book of kids' JOKES

the monster book of
kids' JOKES

ARCTURUS

ARCTURUS

This edition published in 2008 by Arcturus Publishing Limited
26/27 Bickels Yard, 151–153 Bermondsey Street,
London SE1 3HA

ISBN: 978-1-84837-174-3

Illustrations by Peter Coupe

Printed in Singapore

Contents

SCHOOL STUFF

What do you call someone who greets you
at the school door every morning?

Matt!

Teacher - Jenkins, give me a sentence
with the word 'detention' in it !

Jenkins - I had to leave the horror film before it
had finished, because I couldn't stand detention !

★

Smith - Sir, my parents want me to tell you that they were
really pleased with my last report.

Teacher - But I said you were a complete idiot !

Smith - But it's the first time anyone in
our family has been really good at something !

Five good reasons to go to school...

1. Even school dinners are better than my dad's !

2. The heating goes off at home at 9 o'clock !

3. You learn to be independent -
by doing as you're told !

4. The DVD rental shop doesn't open 'til 4 o'clock !

5. You learn what life will be like when you are old
and grumpy - by watching the teachers at
break time!

Where would you find giant snails ?

At the end of giants' fingers !

Head - What do you think about in the school holidays ?

Pupil - I never think about schoolwork !

Head - Not really much of a change for you then ?

★

Head - Mr Snurge, why have you put the school orchestra into the school freezer ?

Mr Snurge - They said they wanted to play some music that was a little more cool !

For tonight's homework I want you to write an essay on a goldfish.

I can't do that Sir !

Why on earth not ?

I don't have any waterproof ink !

I'm not really interested in maths - I just go along to the lesson to make up the numbers !

★

Teacher - Name a bird that doesn't build its own nest.

Arnold - The cuckoo.

Teacher - That's right - how on earth did you know that ?

Arnold - Everyone knows that cuckoos live in clocks !

Did you hear about...

The P.E. teacher who used
to run round the exam
room in the hope of jogging
pupils' memories ?

The maths teacher and the
art teacher who used to
go out together painting
by numbers ?

The craft teacher who
used to have
the class in stitches ?

The science teacher who was
scared of
little glass dishes
- he was petrified ?

The cookery teacher who
thought Hamlet was an
omelette served with bacon ?

★

Why did the school canteen hire a dentist ?

To make more filling meals !

I banged my head on my locker door this morning !

Have you seen the school nurse ?

No, just stars !

Head - Why were you sent out of the
tennis class today ?

Pupil - For making a racket !

★

Teacher - Jones, what were people wearing
during the Great Fire of London ?

Jones - Blazers and smoking jackets ?

Teacher - Who can tell me which sea creature eats
its prey two at a time ?

Pupil - Noah's shark !

★

Teacher - Did you find the exam questions easy ?

Pupil - Oh, yes I found the questions all right, it's the
answers I couldn't find !

★

Teacher - Who was Thor ?

Pupil - The god who kept thcratching hith thpots !

★

Teacher - Sarah, what evidence is there that
smoking is harmful to health ?

Sarah - Well, just look what happened
to all the dragons !

Teacher - Why were you late this morning, Veronica ?

Veronica - I squeezed the toothpaste too hard
and it took me half an hour to get it all back
into the tube again !

Teacher - Ali, if five cats were on
a bus and one got off, how many would be left ?

Ali - None, sir !

Teacher - How do you get that answer ?

Ali - Because the other four
were copycats !

15

Teacher - Weber, I do wish you would pay a little attention !

Weber - I'm paying as little as I can, sir !

Why is Frankenstein's monster rubbish at school ?

He hasn't got the brains he was born with !

Teacher - Robinson, where are you from ?

Robinson - London.

Teacher - Which part ?

Robinson - All of me !

★

What's the difference between a bird watcher and a teenager ?

One gets a hide and spots, the other gets a spot and hides !

Teacher - Mary, why was no-one able to play cards on Noah's Ark ?

Mary - Because Noah stood on the deck !

Teacher - Did you know that most accidents happen in the kitchen ?

Pupil - Yes, but we still have to eat them !

John - Dad, have we got a ladder ?

Dad - What do you need that for ?

John - For homework I have to write an essay on an elephant !

English teacher - Did anyone help you
write this poem, Carol ?

Carol - No, Miss.

English teacher - Well, I'm delighted to meet
you at last, Mr Shakespeare !

Teacher - Stevens, name an ancient musical instrument.

Stevens - An Anglo - saxophone ?

What is a good pet for small children ?

A rattlesnake ??

Why does our robot
teacher never get sick ?

Because he has a cast-
iron constitution !

Teacher - What's the
difference between a
horse and an elephant ?

Pupil - A horse doesn't look
like an elephant !

Teacher - Jarvis, tell me a sentence with the
word 'counterfeit' in it.

Jarvis - I wasn't sure if she was a centipede or
a millipede so I had to counterfeit !

Teacher - Thompson, how would you discover
what life in Ancient Egypt was really like ?

Thompson - I'd ask my mummy !

The Deputy Head is a funny chap,
who creeps from class to class.
He has a face that could curdle cream
and a voice like broken glass !

What's the difference between a school
and a headmaster's car ?

One breaks up, the other breaks down !

How do you cure lockjaw ?

Swallow a key !

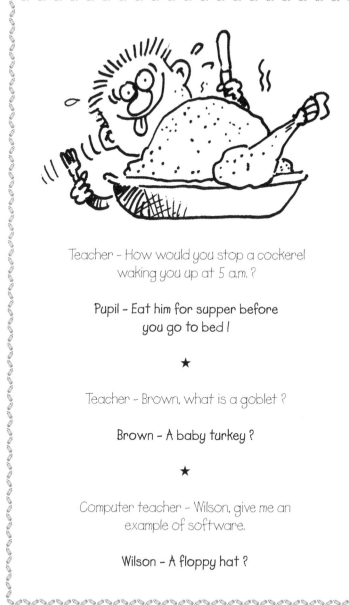

Teacher - How would you stop a cockerel
waking you up at 5 a.m. ?

Pupil - Eat him for supper before
you go to bed !

Teacher - Brown, what is a goblet ?

Brown - A baby turkey ?

Computer teacher - Wilson, give me an
example of software.

Wilson - A floppy hat ?

★ NEW BOOKS IN THE GEOGRAPHY LIBRARY ★

RICE GROWING IN CHINA by **Paddy Fields**

AFRICAN SAFARI by **Rhoda Lion**

EXPLORING SPACE by **Honor Rocket**

THE FROZEN WASTES by **S. Keemo**

CLIMBING EVEREST by **Percy Veerance**

★

Do you know what will happen if you forget to do
your homework for our music teacher ?

You'll find yourself in serious treble !

We love our school
we really do,
we love our lessons
and teachers too!

We love the exams
and the tricky tests,
we love the school dinners
and the P.E. vests !

But why do I sound
so cheerful today?
Because we just started
the summer holidays !

Why did the boy throw his watch out of the window
in the history exam ?

He wanted to make time fly !

Teacher - Gerard, what's a computer byte ?

Gerard - I didn't even know they had teeth !

Teacher - Who discovered Pluto ?

Pupil - Walt Disney ?

Why are teachers like doctors ?

Because they are both good at examinations !

ANIMAL SCHOOL REPORTS...

Cheetah - A nice enough boy, but not to be trusted !

Leopard - Has missed a lot of classes
this year due to spots !

Hyena - Seems to think that everything is a joke !

Stick Insect - Never been the same since the elephant
mistook him for a pencil !

Teacher - Why were you so late for school
this morning ?

Pupil - Oh, did I miss something ?

★

Did you hear about the music teacher who kept
forgetting her register ?!

A bottle of lemonade went to teacher training college – what subject was he going to teach ?

Fizzical education !

A butterfly went to teacher training college – what subject was she going to teach ?

Moth - a - matics !

My music teacher said I have a heavenly voice !

That's not strictly true – she said your voice was like nothing on earth !

Your daughter has the ability to really go places
and, as her teacher, I can't wait !

Our art teacher draws her own conclusions !

Teacher – Are you really going to leave school at
the end of this term, Samantha...or are you just saying
it to cheer me up ?"

Pupil – Ugh! There's a fly in my soup !

Kitchen assistant – Don't worry, the spider
on your bread will get it !

Teacher - I hope I didn't see you cheating
then, Walsh !

Walsh - I hope you didn't see me
cheating either, Miss !

★

You have a photographic memory Blenkinsop,
it's a shame that nothing ever develops !

★

A snail was mugged by two tortoises. He went to the
police, who asked him to describe them.

"I can't," said the snail, "it all happened so fast !"

Teacher - It's clear that you haven't done your geography homework. What's your excuse ?

Pupil - Well, my dad says the world is changing every day, so I decided to wait until it settles down !

Little monster - I hate my teacher !

Mother monster - Well just eat your salad up then dear!

Mother – Why did you just swallow the money I gave you ?

Son – Well you did say it was my lunch money !

Teacher - You copied from John's exam paper didn't you ?

Pupil - How did you know ?

Teacher - John's paper says 'I don't know' and you have put 'Me, neither' !

Father - Why did you get such a low score
in that test ?

Son - Absence.

Father - You were absent on the
day of the test ?

Son - No, but the boy who sits next
to me was !

What kinds of tests do they give witches ?

Hex - aminations !

Teacher - What is an island?

Pupil - A piece of land surrounded by water
except on one side.

Teacher - On one side?

Pupil - Yes, on top!

Mother – How was your first day at school?

Son - It was all right except for some man
called 'Sir' who kept spoiling all our fun!

School cook - What's wrong with
your school dinner?

Pupil - Can you describe it for me please in case
I need to tell my doctor later what I've eaten!

Mother - What was the first thing you
learned in class?

Daughter - How to talk without moving my lips!

Teacher - Can you tell me where elephants
are found ?

Pupil - We don't have to find elephants...
they're so big, they don't get lost !

Teacher - Name an animal that lives in Lapland.

Pupil - A reindeer.

Teacher - Good, now name another.

Pupil - Another reindeer !

What did the computer do at lunchtime ?

Had a byte !

Pupil - I don't think I deserved zero
on this test.

Teacher - I agree, but that's the lowest
mark I could give you !

CRAZY NAMES

What do you call a man with a
car number plate on his head?

Reg!

What do you call a man with a sack, a long white beard and a sleigh?

Bjorn, the oldest postman in Iceland!

★

What do you call a monkey who is king of the jungle?

Henry the Ape!

★

What do you call a woman with a frog on her head?

Lily!

★

What do you call a man who lives in Scotland?

Glen!

★

What do you call a woman with a shotgun in her hand?

Whatever she tells you to, or else!

What name do you give a dog
that likes to wander off all the time ?

Rover !

What do you call the Roman Emperor who
kept pet mice ?

Julius Cheeser !

What do you call a man with a horse's head ?

Nathan !

What do you call a woman who sells parrots ?

Polly !

What do you call an Irishman sitting on a verandah ?

Paddy O'Furniture !

What do you call a woman who was eaten
by her cannibal husband ?

Henrietta !

What was the name of the man who designed King
Arthur's round table ?

Sir Cumference !

What do you call a man who owns a seaside
sweet factory ?

Rock !

What do you call a man with his head in an oven ?

Stew !

★

What do you call an Ancient Egyptian
with no teeth ?

A gummy mummy !

★

What do you call a man with a tissue paper head ?

Russell !

★

What do you call a failed lion tamer ?

Claude Bottom !

★

What do you call a frightened man ?

Hugo First !

What do you call a
man with a bowl of
porridge on his head?

Scott!

★

What do you call a
man with an oil well
on his head?

Derek!

★

What do you call a man who lifts
cars up in a garage?

Jack!

★

What do you call a dog that is a always
rushing about?

A dash - hound!

What do you call a girl with a huge plate of food?

Anita!

What do you call a woman with
a plant pot on her head?

Rose!

What do you call a man with very
strong spectacles?

Seymore!

What do you call a man who delivers
Christmas presents to lions and tigers ?

Santa Claws !

★

What do you call a man who doesn't sink ?

Bob !

★

What do you call a woman who knows
where she lives ?

Olivia !

What do you call a man with money on his head ?

Bill !

What do you call a man with a
duck on his head ?

Donald !

What do you call a woman who
works at the zoo ?

Ellie Fant !

What do you call a man with three eyes ?

Seymour !

What do you call a woman with a ball of
wool on her head ?

Barbara Blacksheep !

What did the Spaniard call his first
and only son ?

Juan !

What do you call a man with a springboard on his head ?

Jim !

What do you call a girl who comes out
very early in the morning ?

Dawn !

What do you call a man with a male cat on his head ?

Tom !

What do you call a man with a small pig on his head ?

Hamlet !

What do you call a man with a
stolen safe on his head?

Robin Banks!

What do you call the illness that martial
arts experts catch?

Kung flu!

What do you call a Tyrannosaurus Rex that won't stop talking?

A dino - bore!

What do you call a boy with no shins?

Tony!

What do you call a woman who plays pool with a pint of beer on her head?

Beatrix Potter!

What do you call a lion with toothache?

Rory!

What do you call a play acted by ghosts?

A phantomime!

What do you call a man with a box of
treasure on his head?

Chester!

What do you call a woman with a
sinking ship on her head?

Mandy Lifeboats!

What do you call a woman with a
pyramid on her head?

Mummy!

What do you call a girl with a
head made of sugar?

Candy!

What do you call a girl with a head made of glass?

Crystal!

What do you call a man with a wooden head?

Edward!

What do you call a woman with
two toilets on her head ?

Lulu !

What do you call a girl with a head made of honey ?

Bee - trix !

What do you call a man carrying legal documents ?

Will !

What do you call a man with a fire on his head ?

Ashley !

What do you call a man with a
jumbo jet parked on his head ?

Ron Way !

What do you call a girl with an
orange on her head?

Clementine!

What do you call a man in a bull-fighting ring?

Gord!

What do you call a man with turf on his head?

Pete!

What do you call a man with a school
register on his head?

Mark!

What do you call a woman with a doll on her head?

Sindy!

What do you call a woman with
a boat tied to her head?

Maude!

What do you call a man with a
heavy goods vehicle on his head?

Laurie!

What do you call a woman with a
tub of butter on her head?

Marge!

What do you call a girl with flowers growing out of her head?

Daisy!

What do you call a man with a vegetable patch on his head?

Mr Bean!

What do you call a woman with a badly-fitted head?

Lucy!

What do you call a man with a spade
sticking out of his head?

Doug!

What do you call a man without a spade
sticking out of his head?

Douglas!

What do you call a cow that lives in the Arctic?

An eskimoo!

What do you call a cat that lives in an igloo?

An eskimew!

What do you call a cat that was caught by the police?

The purrpatrator!

What do you a man with a pair of
spectacles on his head ?

Luke !

★

What do you call a woman with a
kettle on her head ?

Polly !
(Well, in the nursery rhyme
Polly Put The Kettle On !)

★

What do you call a man with a
sprig of holly on his head ?

Buddy !

What do you call a man with a large,
fiery object on his head?

Sonny!

What do you call a cow with no legs?

Ground beef!

What do you call a woman with some
thin paper and a pencil on her head?

Tracey!

What do you call a woman with
half a lizard on her head?

Liz!

What do you call a spaceship made from cowpats?

A poo F O

What do you call a criminal with
a fish down his trousers ?

The Codfather !

★

What do you call a girl with a bucket
and spade on her head ?

Sandy !

What do you call a man with a used
postage stamp on his head ?

Frank !

What do you call a crate of ducks ?

A box of quackers !

What do you call a happy mushroom ?

Fun Gus !

What do you call a woman with a plate of
food on her head ?

Amelia !

What do you call a vampire with
a calculator on his head ?

The Count !

What do you call a boomerang that doesn't work ?

A stick !

What do you call a teacher with
a joke book on his head ?

A tee - hee - cher !

What do you call a pig doing karate ?

A pork chop !

What do you call a man with a
pile of chopped firewood on his head ?

Axel !

What do you call two spiders who have just
got married ?

Newly-webs !

What do you call a man with an
anvil on his head?

Smith!

What do you call a dog that's
always snapping at people?

Camera!

What do you call a fat space alien ?

An extra - cholesterol !

What do you call a man with some cheese on his head ?

Gordon Zola !

What do you call a woman with a steering wheel on her head ?

Carmen !

What do you call a new, super cat ?

A mew improved version !

What do you call a hippo that wears flowers in its hair and beads around its neck ?

A hippie - potamus !

What do you call Santa's wife ?

Mary Christmas !

What do you call a man who used to like farm machinery ?

An ex - tractor fan !

What do you call a cow's favourite city ?

Moo York !

What do you call a dinosaur that wears a cowboy hat and boots ?

Tyrannosaurus Tex !

★

What do you call a sheepdog with a bunch of daisies on its head ?

Collie Flower !

What do you call a country where everyone
has to drive a red car ?

A red carnation !

What do you call a country where everyone
has to drive a pink car ?

A pink carnation !

What do you call a judge with no thumbs?

Justice Fingers !

What do you call a party for snowmen ?

A snowball !

What do you call a really small woman ?

Dot !

What do you call a flying woman?

Rose !

★

What do you call a woman setting fire to outstanding bills?

Bernadette!

What do you call a man at the side of a house?

Ali !

What do you call a woman who
sings at Christmas ?

Carol !

What do you call someone drilling holes in
a piece of wood ?

Boring !

What do you call a man with a raincoat ?

Mac !

What do you call a man with a large raincoat ?

Big Mac !

What do you call a man with two raincoats ?

Max !

ANIMAL MADNESS

What sweet do lambs like best ?

A big baaaaa of chocolate !

On Christmas Eve a married couple were looking up into the sky at something travelling towards them.

"Is it a snow storm?" asked the wife.

The husband replied, "No, it looks like reindeer!"

What do you do if an elephant sits in front of you at the cinema?

Miss the film!

What did the Pink Panther say when he stood on an ant?

Dead ant, dead ant,
dead ant dead ant dead ant...

What do elephants take to help them sleep?

Trunkquilisers!

Where do tadpoles change into frogs?

In the croakroom!

What did the dog say when it sat on some sandpaper?

Ruff!

What do you call a delinquent octopus?

A crazy, mixed-up squid!

What is the most cowardly farmyard creature ?

A chicken !

★

What is the cheapest way to hire a horse ?

Stand it on four bricks !

★

What is the tallest yellow flower in the world ?

A giraffodil !

What sort of bird steals from banks ?

A robin !

★

What is green and white and hops ?

An escaping frog sandwich !

★

Why is an elephant like a teacher ?

Put a tack on an elephants chair
and you'll soon find out !

What do you call a stupid elephant with his
own aeroplane ?

A dumbo jet !

Mary had a little lamb
the lamb began to tease her.
"Stop it," she said. The lamb refused
and now it's in the freezer !

★

Why did the lettuce blush ?

Because it saw the salad dressing !

What do you call a large grey animal that's
just eaten a ton of beans?

A smellyphant!

What do you get if you cross a hunting dog
with a newspaper writer?

A newshound!

What sort of horse does a ghost ride ?

A night - mare !

How do ducks play tennis ?

With a quacket !

Why do bears have fur coats ?

Because they can't get plastic macs
in their size !

Where is the hottest place in the jungle ?

Under a gorilla !

Where do horses sit when they go
to the theatre ?

In the stalls !

What is big and grey and good at sums?

An elephant with a calculator!

★

Two cows were talking in a field...

First cow - Are you worried about catching this mad cow disease?

Second cow - Baaaa!

Why did the chicken run out onto the football pitch?

Because the referee whistled for a fowl!

Why did the chicken cross the playground?

To get to the other slide!

What ballet stars pigs?

Swine Lake!

What do you do with a green elephant?

Wait until he's ripe!

What happened to the frog's car
when it broke down ?

It was toad away !

Good morning Mr Butcher - do you
have pigs' trotters ?

No, I always walk like this !

What do sheep use to get clean ?

A baaaa of soap !

What says moo, baaa, woof, quack, meeooow, oink ?

A sheep that speaks foreign languages !

★

What flu-ridden animals do the police use ?

Sniffer dogs !

★

What do you get if you cross a
crazy dog and a sheep ?

Something that's baaaarrking mad !

What is the best way to get in touch with a fish ?

Drop him a line !

★

What do you get if you cross a pig with a millipede ?

Bacon and legs !

★

Where would you find a Martian milking a cow ?

In the milky way !

Why do elephants have trunks ?

Because they would never fit their huge
clothes into a suitcase !

★

When do lions have
twelve feet ?

When there are
three of them !

★

First leopard - Hey, is that
a jogger over there ?

Second leopard - Yes,
great, I love fast food !

★

Johnny - Mum, is our dog metric ?

Mum - Why do you ask ?

Johnny - Because Dad said it has just had a
litre of puppies !

What is round, brown, smelly and plays music ?

A cowpat on a record player !

What is black and white and gets
complaints from all the neighbours ?

A zebra learning to play the drums !

★

How can you get eggs without chickens ?

By keeping geese and ducks !

Why should you be naughty if you have
a cow for a teacher ?

**Because if you are good you might
get a pat on the head !**

First goldfish - I told you we'd be famous one day
and now it's going to come true !

**Second goldfish - Wow! When is all this going
to happen ?**

First goldfish - They're putting us on the
television tomorrow !

What is a polygon ?

An escaped parrot !

Where do cows go for their holidays?

Patagonia!

I've lost my dog!!

Why don't you put an advert in the newspaper?

Don't be stupid - he can't read!

Who cuts a sheep's hair ?

The baaarber !

Where do farm animals keep their savings ?

In a piggy bank !

Why do octopuses never get mugged ?

Because they are always well-armed !

What did the idiot call his pet zebra ?

Spot !

Why are cows rubbish at maths ?

Because they haven't invented the cowculator yet !

What is it called when a cat falls from the roof and smashes into the greenhouse ?

A catastrophe !

What do you call an insect that has forgotten the words to a song ?

A humbug !

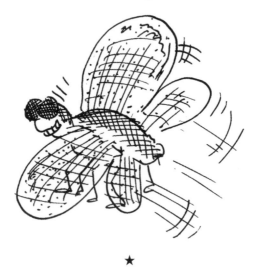

What game do skunks like to play ?

Ping pong !

★

What was the first motorised vegetable called ?

The horseless cabbage !

Why was the man looking for a 30-metre tall Monopoly box in the jungle?

He was a big game hunter!

★

Where are all the aspirins in the jungle?

There aren't any - the paracetamol!

★

What do cats read over breakfast?

The mewspaper!

How do frogs send messages to each other?

By morse toad!

★

What do cows eat for breakfast?

Moosli!

Why do some animals wear cowboy boots in the jungle?

Because they go lion dancing!

What is the first thing Tarzan puts on in the morning?

His jungle pants!

Why don't leopards bother to cheat in exams?

Because they know that they will always be spotted!

Why was the zebra put in charge of the jungle army?

Because he had the most stripes!

What do country and western singers wear in the jungle?

Rhino - stones!

What is smelly and has no sense of humour ?

A dead hyena !

★

I'd like a pair of gloves for my dog, please.

What breed is he ?

A boxer !

★

What do you call a well-dressed jungle cat ?

A dandy lion !

Where does a horse stay on holiday ?

In the bridle suite !

How do sheep buy and sell things ?

They have a baaarter system !

Why did the sheep buy a pub ?

He's always wanted to own a baaa !

What sort of music do you hear most in the jungle?

Snake, rattle and roll!

What do cows put on in the morning?

Udder pants!

How do you control a horse?

Bit by bit!

Why was the young horse sent out of
the classroom?

He was acting the foal!

What was the name of the horse that
fought windmills ?

Donkey Oatey !

★

What sort of jokes do chickens like best ?

Corny ones !

★

Who is a dog's favourite comedian ?

Growlcho Marx !

Where do cats go when they die ?

The purrr - ly gates of heaven !

Where do rodents go for their holidays ?

Hamster Dam !

Doctor, doctor, I'm turning into a young cat!

You must be kitten me!

What is the difference between a buffalo and a bison?

You can't wash your hands in a buffalo!

What sort of flowers do monkeys grow?

Chimp - pansies!

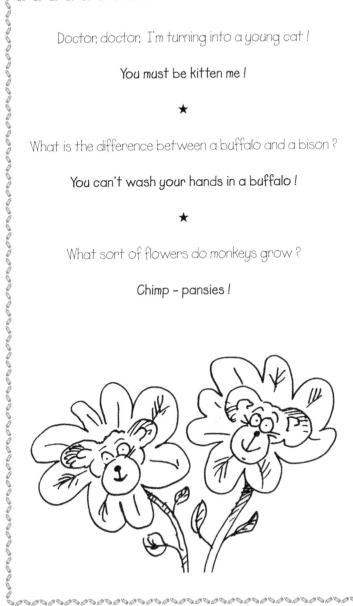

When cows play football, who has the whistle ?

The heiferee !

★

Why don't farmers allow sheep to learn karate ?

Because their chops would be too hard !

★

What do you get if you cross a tortoise with a bird ?

A turtle dove !

Why don't elephants use computers ?

Because they are scared of the mouse !

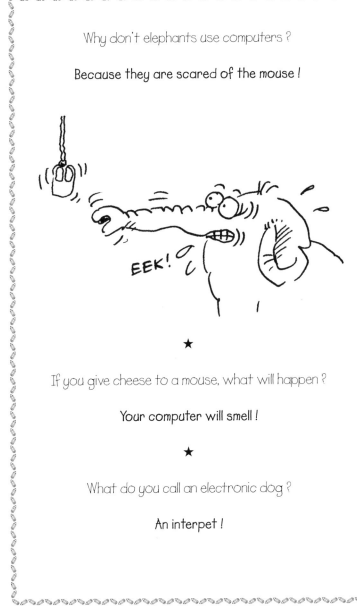

★

If you give cheese to a mouse, what will happen ?

Your computer will smell !

★

What do you call an electronic dog ?

An interpet !

What was the name of the famous French cow painter?

Too moos Lautrec!

What does a sheep call members of his family?

Sheepskin!

What do sheep do on sunny days?

Have a baa baa cue!

Why don't cows sunbathe?

Because they don't want to tan their hides!

What is it called when an insect kills itself?

Insecticide!

What was the name of the woman who successfully crossed the Gobi desert?

Rhoda Camel!

What grows down as it grows up?

A goose!

What do you get if you cross a baby with a porcupine?

A lot of problems changing nappies!

Why did the astronaut jump onto the cow's back?

He wanted to be the first man on the moo!

My daughter took her pet sheep to
the local sports day.

"Is he a good jumper?" someone asked her.

"Not yet," she replied!

What do you call an elephant that's also a witch doctor?

A mumbo - jumbo!

Why are elephants such bad dancers?

Because they have two left feet!

What did the first piranha say to the second?

I've got a bone to pick with you!

Why do bat mums and dads always
complain about their kids?

Because all they do is hang around all day!

★

Which creature builds all the houses
in the jungle?

The boa - constructor!

What did the boa constrictor say to the explorer ?

I've got a crush on you !

★

What do you do if you fancy a bite in the jungle ?

Kick a lion !

★

Which bird is good at chess ?

The rook !

What lives in gum trees ?

Stick insects !

Why is it hard to fool a stick insect ?

Because they always twig !

Why did the stick insect go to university ?

He wanted to branch out !

★

Two baby skunks - called In and Out - went out for
a walk one day. In got lost, but his brother
soon found him. How ?

In - stinkt !

What does a pig use for writing ?

Pen and oink !

What do you call a pig with three eyes ?

Piiig !

What do you call a thieving pig ?

A hamburglar !

Why did the idiot take some
ketchup to the zoo ?

**To put on the
chippopotamus !**

★

Why do cats always
finish the job ?

Because they purr - severe !

★

What jumps up and down in front of a car ?

Froglights !

★

Why was the frog down in the mouth ?

He was unhoppy !

★

Where do fish keep their money ?

In a river bank !

How would you sell a cow's home ?

You would need to find a byre !

★

What did the farmer say when someone
asked him if he had any hay ?

Yes, stacks !

What sort of music does a
gifted rodent write ?

Mouseterpieces !

Baby snake - Dad, are we poisonous ?

Dad snake - No, son, why do you ask ?

Baby snake - I've just bitten my tongue !

What do you get if you cross a kangaroo with a kilt ?

Hop Scotch !

What do you give a budgie with constipation ?

Chirrup of figs !

What did the well-mannered sheep say to his friend at the field gate ?

After ewe !

What looks like half a cat ?

The other half !

What was the name of the film about a killer lion that swam underwater ?

'Claws' !

If a four-legged animal is a quadruped and a two-legged animal is a biped, what's a tiger ?

A stri-ped !

What do you get if you cross a cat with a tree ?

A cat - a - logue !

What flies around your light at night and can
bite off your head ?

A tiger moth !

What does the lion say to his friends before they
go out hunting for food ?

"Let us prey !"

What do you call a cat with eight legs that
likes to swim ?

An octopuss !

Why did the poor dog chase his own tail ?

He was trying to make ends meet !

What do you call a dog with no legs ?

It doesn't matter, he still won't come !

What is a sheep's favourite wine ?

Lambrusco !

What kind of fish do pelicans like ?

Any kind - as long as they fit the bill !

What is sheepskin useful for ?

Keeping the sheep's insides where they belong !

How do fireflies start a race ?

Ready, steady, glow !

Why do farmers
keep cows ?

**Because there are no
udder animals as good
at giving milk !**

★

How do elephants change
their car wheels if
they have a puncture ?

**They lift it up with
a jackal !**

★

How do you stop a skunk
from smelling ?

Tie a knot in his nose !

★

"I think I just heard an owl."

**"You probably did. I just stepped on
the dog's foot !"**

What bird is always running out of breath?

The puffin!

Where do fish wash?

In a river basin!

Why did the lizard go on a diet?

It weighed too much for its scales!

What creature sticks to the bottom of sheep ships ?

Baaa - nacles !

★

What's the difference between a well-dressed
man and a tired dog ?

One wears a suit and the other just pants !

★

How do you stop moles digging up your garden ?

Hide the spades !

★

What kind of bull doesn't have horns ?

A bullfrog !

What is the difference between a fly and a bird?

A bird can fly but a fly can't bird!

What's the difference between a rabbit and
a lumberjack?

One chews and hops, the other
hews and chops!

What's a toad's favourite ballet?

Swamp Lake!

What kind of bee always drops things?

A fumble bee!

What's green and can jump a mile a minute?

A frog with hiccups!

How do you post a bunny?

By hare mail !

What is a bunny's motto ?

Don't be mad, be hoppy !

What fish only swims at night ?

A starfish !

★

How do you know carrots are good for your eyes ?

Because you never see rabbits wearing glasses !

KNOCK, KNOCK...

Knock, Knock...
Who's there ?
Carmen
Carmen who ?
Carmen to the front room and
look through the window !

Knock, knock...
Who's there?
Mort
Mort who?
Mort have known you would ask me that!

Knock, Knock...
Who's there?
Don
Don who?
Don worry - I'm not a burglar!

Knock, Knock...
Who's there?
Acton
Acton who?
Acton stupid won't do you any good!

Knock, Knock...
Who's there?
Barker
Barker who?
**Barker door's locked so I've come
round to the front!**

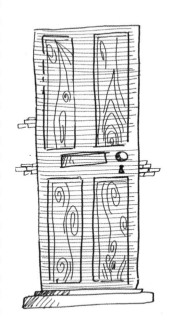

Knock, Knock...
Who's there ?
Carrie
Carrie who ?
**Carrie this shopping in for
me, it weighs a ton !**

Knock, Knock...
Who's there ?
It's Jilly
It's Jilly who ?
It's Jilly out here – let me in !

Knock, Knock...
Who's there ?
Eddie
Eddie who ?
Eddie minute now I'm going to sneeze !

Knock, Knock...
Who's there ?
Fred
Fred who ?
Fred you'll have to open the door to find out !

Knock, Knock...
Who's there ?
Geoff
Geoff who ?
Geoff to ask that question every single time ?

Knock, Knock...
Who's there ?
Harry
Harry who ?
Harry up it's just starting to rain !

Knock, Knock...
Who's there ?
Iona
Iona who ?
Iona a house just like this one !

Knock, Knock...
Who's there ?
Ken
Ken who ?
Ken you not guess ?

Knock, Knock...
Who's there ?
June
June who ?
June know how long I've been waiting out here ?

Knock, Knock...
Who's there ?
Can you Linda
Can you Linda who ?
Can you Linda cup of sugar ?

★

Knock, Knock...
Who's there ?
Oscar
Oscar who ?
Oscar nother question for goodness sake !

Knock, Knock...
Who's there ?
Pete
Pete who ?
Pete after me, "I am going to open the door now...!"

Knock, Knock...
Who's there ?
Ronnie
Ronnie who ?
Ronnie nose - need a tissue, quick !

Knock, Knock...
Who's there ?
Stella
Stella who ?
Stella same person who was here last time you asked !

Knock, Knock...
Who's there ?
Tone
Tone who ?
Tone keep asking me that same old question !

Knock, Knock...
Who's there ?
Unger
Unger who ?
Unger the doormat is where you'll find the key !

★

Knock, Knock...
Who's there ?
Val
Val who ?
Val how am I supposed to know ?!

Knock, Knock...
Who's there ?
Wanda
Wanda who ?
Wanda know? Then open the door and find out !

Knock, Knock...
Who's there?
Xavier
Xavier who?
Xavier anything for the
jumble sale?

Knock, Knock...
Who's there?
Annie
Annie who?
Annie chance you'll open
this door?

Knock, Knock...
Who's there?
Carla
Carla who?
Carla doctor, your door knocker has
just fallen off and broken my toe!

Knock, Knock...
Who's there ?
Barbara
Barbara who ?
Barbara Blacksheep !

★

Knock, Knock...
Who's there ?
Deb
Deb who ?
**Deb better be a good reason for keeping
me waiting out here !**

Knock, Knock...
Who's there ?
Emma
Emma who ?
Emma not going to tell you again !

Knock, Knock...
Who's there ?
Fanny
Fanny who ?
Fanny how you always ask that question...!

Knock, Knock...
Who's there ?
Arthur
Arthur who ?
Arthur gotten again !

Knock, Knock...
Who's there ?
Eileen Dover
Eileen Dover who ?
Eileen Dover your fence and broke it !

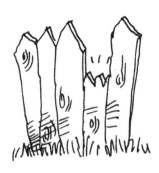

Knock, Knock...
Who's there ?
Herbert
Herbert who ?
**Herbert you come to the door and
see for yourself !**

★

Knock, Knock...
Who's there ?
Morse
Morse who ?
Morse come in as quickly as possible !

Knock, Knock...
Who's there ?
Nipper
Nipper who ?
**Nipper round the back and
pass my spectacles !**

Knock, Knock...
Who's there ?
Oscar
Oscar who ?
Oscar a silly question...

Knock, Knock...
Who's there ?
Quad
Quad who ?
Quad you want to know for ?

Knock, Knock...
Who's there ?
Sandy
Sandy who ?
Sandy you living next door, isn't it ?

Knock, Knock...
Who's there ?
Russell
Russell who ?
Russell be home in a minute - put the kettle on !

Knock, Knock...
Who's there ?
Tamara
Tamara who ?
Tamara's my birthday, don't forget !

★

Knock, Knock...
Who's there ?
Urquart
Urquart who ?
Urquart just broke down, can you call the garage ?

Knock, Knock...
Who's there ?
Vera
Vera who ?
Vera long way from home and need a map !

Knock, Knock...
Who's there ?
Wendy
Wendy who ?
Wendy door finally opens you can
see for yourself !

Knock, Knock...
Who's there ?
Xara
Xara who ?
Xara front door the same colour as this yesterday !

Knock, Knock...
Who's there ?
Miguel
Miguel who ?
Miguel friend's dumped me !

Knock, Knock...
Who's there ?
Euripides
Euripides who ?
Euripides trousers, you'll have to buy some more !

Knock, Knock...
Who's there ?
Ben
Ben who ?
Ben down the supermarket, give us a hand with
these bags !

Knock, Knock...
Who's there ?
Clara
Clara who ?
**Clara space for the shopping bags
like Ben told you to !**

Knock, Knock...
Who's there ?
Lucy
Lucy who ?
Lucy Lastic !

Knock, Knock...
Who's there ?
Paul
Paul who ?
Paul the other one, it's got bells on !

129

Knock, Knock...
Who's there ?
John
John who ?
John know I'm getting tired standing out here !

Knock, Knock...
Who's there ?
Moore
Moore who ?
Moore or less the same person as before !

Knock, Knock...
Who's there ?
Julienne
Julienne who ?
Julienne against that front door all day ?

Knock, Knock...
Who's there ?
Carter
Carter who ?
Carter pillar !

Knock, Knock...
Who's there ?
Toulouse
Toulouse who ?
Toulouse are better than one in a busy house,
I always say !

Knock, Knock...
Who's there ?
Double glazing salesman....hello...hello...

★

Knock, Knock...
Who's there ?
Furze
Furze who ?
Furze I'm concerned you can keep the door closed !

Knock, Knock...
Who's there ?
Germaine
Germaine who ?
Germaine I can't come in unless I tell you ?

Knock, Knock...
Who's there ?
Mush
Mush who ?
Mush you always ask me this ?

Knock, Knock...
Who's there ?
Mandy
Mandy who ?
Mandy Lifeboats !

Knock, Knock...
Who's there ?
Frank
Frank who ?
Frank you for asking !

Knock, Knock...
Who's there ?
Egon
Egon who ?
Egon down the shops !

Knock, Knock...
Who's there ?
Harmony
Harmony who ?
Harmony times do I have to tell you ?!

SIGH..

Knock, Knock...
Who's there ?
Sitter
Sitter who ?
Sitter good time to come round ?

★

Knock, Knock...
Who's there ?
Don
Don who ?
Don be afraid...look into my eyes...
you are feeling sleepy...

★

Knock, Knock...
Who's there ?
Ma
Ma who ?
Ma car broke down again !

★

Knock, Knock...
Who's there ?
A guest
A guest who ?
A guest you wouldn't recognise my voice !

Knock, Knock...
Who's there ?
Dan
Dan who ?
Dan Dan Dan Dan Daaaannnn !

Knock, Knock...
Who's there ?
Moses
Moses who ?
**Moses you have to let me in without asking
stupid questions !**

Knock, Knock...
Who's there ?
Carrie
Carrie who ?
**Carrie on like this
and I'll freeze to
death out here !**

135

Knock, Knock...
Who's there ?
Hal
Hal who ?
Halloo !

★

Knock, Knock...
Who's there ?
A ghost
A ghost who ?
**Thought it would
scare you !**

★

Knock, Knock...
Who's there ?
Kenya
Kenya who ?
Kenya please just open the door ?

★

Knock, Knock...
Who's there ?
France
France who ?
France-y meeting you here !

Knock, Knock...
Who's there ?
Adolf
Adolf who ?
Adolf ball hit me in de mouf !

★

Knock, Knock...
Who's there ?
Chris
Chris who ?
Chris Packet, but my friends call me Russell !

Knock, Knock...
Who's there ?
Iona
Iona who ?
Iona have eyes for you !

Knock, Knock...
Who's there ?
Tinkerbell
Tinkerbell who ?
Tinkerbell would look nice on my bike ?

★

Knock, Knock...
Who's there ?
Maquis
Maquis who ?
Maquis just snapped in the lock !

Knock, Knock...
Who's there?
Jethro
Jethro who?
Jethro people out if they can't pay their bill?

Knock, Knock...
Who's there?
Ivor
Ivor who?
Ivor message for a Mr Smith!

Knock, Knock...
Who's there ?
Sid
Sid who ?
Sid down next to me !

!Knock, Knock...
Who's there ?
Shirley
Shirley who ?
Shirley you know the sound of my voice by now ?

Knock, Knock...
Who's there ?
Jester
Jester who ?
Jester minute I've forgotten !

Knock, Knock...
Who's there ?
Lettuce
Lettuce who ?
Lettuce in and you'll find out !

★

Knock, Knock...
Who's there ?
Sinbad
Sinbad who ?
Sinbad condition, your front door !

Knock, Knock...
Who's there ?
Harry
Harry who ?
Harry up and let me in !

Knock, Knock...
Who's there ?
Caine
Caine who ?
Caine you see me through the glass ?

Knock, Knock...
Who's there ?
Cattle
Cattle who ?
**Cattle get out if you open the door,
I'll come in through the window !**

Knock, Knock…
Who's there ?
Norma Lee
Norma Lee who ?
Norma Lee I don't go around knocking on doors, but do you want to buy a set of encyclopedias ?

Knock, Knock…
Who's there ?
Tank
Tank who ?
You're welcome!

Knock, Knock…
Who's there ?
Ya
Ya who ?
What are you getting so excited about ?

Knock, Knock…
Who's there ?
Repeat
Repeat who ?
Who who who…

Knock, Knock...
Who's there ?
Who
Who who ?
Have you got an owl in there ?

Knock, Knock...
Who's there ?
Anita
Anita who ?
Anita to borrow a pencil !

Knock, Knock...
Who's there ?
Ice cream
Ice cream who ?
Ice cream every time I see a ghost !

Knock, Knock...
Who's there ?
Omelet
Omelet who ?
Omelet smarter than I look !

Knock, Knock...
Who's there ?
And your old lady
And your old lady who ?
I didn't know you could yodel !

★

Knock, Knock...
Who's there ?
Doris
Doris who ?
Doris closed - that's why I'm having to knock !

Knock, Knock...
Who's there ?
Europe
Europe who ?
Europe bright and early today !

★

Knock, Knock...
Who's there ?
Orang
Orang who ?
Orang the doorbell but it doesn't seem to work, so now I'm knocking !

★

Knock, Knock...
Who's there ?
Alf
Alf who ?
Alf feed the cat while you're on holiday !

Knock, Knock...
Who's there ?
Pecan
Pecan who ?
Pecan someone your own size !

Knock, Knock...
Who's there ?
Annie
Annie who ?
Annie thing you can do, I can do better !

Knock, Knock...
Who's there ?
Police
Police who ?
Police let us in, it's cold out here !

Knock, Knock...
Who's there ?
I love
I love who ?
I don't know, you tell me !

Knock, Knock...
Who's there ?
Stephanie
Stephanie who ?
Stephanie me – who else could it be !

Knock, Knock...
Who's there ?
Wooden shoe
Wooden shoe who ?
Wooden shoe like to know ?

Knock, Knock...
Who's there ?
May-Belle
May-Belle who ?
May-Belle don't work either, so I'm knocking !

Knock, Knock...
Who's there ?
Noah
Noah who ?
Noah a good place to hide from this rain ?

Knock, Knock...
Who's there ?
Will
Will who ?
Will I ever be let in ?

Knock, Knock...
Who's there ?
Luke
Luke who ?
Luke out - the Martians are landing !

Knock, Knock...
Who's there ?
Mindy
Mindy who ?
Mindy porch !

Knock, Knock...
Who's there ?
Othello
Othello who ?
Othello could freeze to death out here !

Knock, Knock...
Who's there ?
Cash
Cash who ?
No, thanks, I'm allergic to nuts !

Knock, Knock...
Who's there ?
Oasis
Oasis who ?
Oasis, it's your brother, I forgot my key !

Knock, Knock...
Who's there ?
Mickey
Mickey who ?
Mickey don't fit - have you changed the locks ?

Knock, Knock...
Who's there ?
Kong
Kong who ?
Kong - ratulations, you've won the lottery !

Knock, Knock...
Who's there ?
Abi
Abi who ?
Abi stung me on the nose !

Knock, Knock...
Who's there ?
Moss
Moss who ?
Moss be time to move onto the next section !

MONSTER MIRTH

What do you call a monster airline steward?

A fright attendant!

Why are monsters always falling out
with each other ?

There's always a bone of contention !

What songs do they play at ghostly discos ?

Haunting melodies !

★

What does a young monster call his parents ?

Mummy and Deady !

What does a baby vampire say before
going to bed ?

Turn on the dark ! I'm afraid of the light !

What is Transylvania ?

Dracula's terror-tory !

What is the largest building in Transylvania ?

The Vampire State Building !

Why did Dracula go to jail ?

Because he robbed the blood bank !

How can you tell when a vampire has
been in a bakery ?

**All the jam has been sucked out
of the doughnuts !**

What are a monster's favourite fairground rides ?

The helter skeleton and the roller ghoster !

★

What did the skeleton say when his
brother told a lie ?

You can't fool me, I can see right through you !

What type of art do skeletons like ?

Skull - tures !

Mum, I've decided I don't like my brother !

Well, just eat the chips and leave him on the side of the plate !

Why was the monster catching centipedes ?

He wanted scrambled legs for breakfast !

What game do ghostly mice play at parties ?

Hide and squeak !

What did the skeleton say while riding his Harley Davidson motorcycle ?

I'm bone to be wild !

Why did the monster buy an axe ?

Because he wanted to get ahead in life !

Why did the monster eat his music teacher ?

His Bach was worse than his bite !

Who was the most famous French skeleton ?

Napoleon Bone-apart !

What kind of monster is safe to put in the
washing machine?

A wash and wear wolf !

What do vampires have at eleven o'clock every day ?

A coffin break !

What kind of girl does a mummy take on a date ?

Any old girl he can dig up !

Why did the mummy leave his tomb after 1,000 years ?

Because he thought it was time he left home !

Why was the monster scared of the computer ?

Because its memory had a kilobyte !

Why do monsters have lots of nightmares ?

They like to take their work to bed with them !

Why should you never touch a monster's tail ?

Because it is the end of the monster, and it could also be the end of you !

What game do young monsters play ?

Corpse and robbers !

What do monsters like to pour on their Sunday dinner ?

Grave - y !

Where do monsters go on their American holidays ?

Death Valley !

How does Frankenstein's monster eat ?

He bolts his food down !

What is a vampire's favourite game ?

Bat-minton !

What is a vampire's favourite fruit ?

A neck-tarine !

Why does Dracula consider himself
to be a good artist ?

Because he likes to draw blood!

Why did the vampire need mouthwash ?

He had bat breath !

Why did the monster comedian like
playing to skeletons ?

Because he knew how to tickle their funny bones !

Why didn't Dracula get married ?

He never met a nice ghoul !

What do you call a monster that comes to
your home to collect your laundry ?

An undie - taker !

What is the first thing a monster does
when you give him an axe ?

Writes out a chopping list !

Which room in your home can ghouls not enter ?

The living room !

Why did the monster have twins in his lunchbox ?

In case he fancied seconds !

What did the mummy monster say to her child
at the dining table ?

Don't spook with your mouth full !

What job could a young monster do ?

Be a chop assistant !

How did the monster cook the local hairdresser ?

On a barber - cue !

What did the metal monster have on his gravestone?

Rust In Peace!

What do monsters have at tea time?

Scream cakes!

SOME MONSTER HOLIDAYS...

Good Fryday!
(Good for frying anyone who gets close
enough to grab!)

Eater Sunday and Eater Monday!
(Monsters don't have eggs!)

Crisps and Eve!
(Another traditional monster recipe!)

What is red, sweet and bites people?

A jampire!

What film did the monster James Bond star in ?

Ghouldfinger !

★

Why didn't the skeleton fight the monster ?

He didn't have the guts !

Where do skeletons keep their money ?

In a joint account !

Why wasn't the naughty ghost afraid of
the police ?

Because he knew they couldn't pin
anything on him !

What do monsters eat if they catch someone
breaking into their home ?

Beef burglers !

What do monsters make with cars ?

Traffic jam !

How many monsters would it take to fill this room ?

No idea, I'd be off after the first one arrived !

What does a skeleton order at a restaurant ?

Spare ribs !

Why are monsters so
horrible ?

It's in the blood !

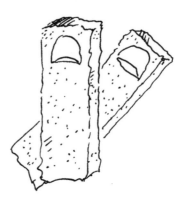

Why do monsters breed
fish with hands ?

So they can have fish
fingers with their chips !

Some foreign countries favoured by monsters...

Eat a Lee !

Belch um !

Gnaw Wayne !

Sweet Den

What do headless monsters eat ?

Chops !

Did you hear about the monster who asked if he could leave the dining table?

His mum said yes, she would put it in the fridge and he could eat it later!

★

Which monster monkey thinks he can sing?

King Song!

Whay do you call a monster with an
axe buried in his head ?

Nothing - it's perfectly normal for monsters !

★

Who patrols the graveyard at night ?

A fright watchman !

★

Why don't mummies go on holiday ?

They're afraid they might relax and unwind !

BARMY BRAIN
TEASERS

Why have you buried my car?

Because the battery is dead!

What did the bull say when he came back
from the china shop ?

I've had a really smashing time !

When do 2 and 2 make more than 4 ?

When they make 22 !

Why were the naughty eggs sent out of the class ?

For playing practical yolks !

Why should you never listen too closely to a match?

Because you might burn your ears!

Why did the bakers work late?

Because they kneaded the dough!

What has 50 legs?

A centipede cut in half!

How does Santa begin a joke?

"This one will sleigh you...!"

★

What jewellery do ghosts wear?

Tombstones!

★

How can you sleep like a log?

Put your bed in the fireplace!

What can you catch and hold but never touch ?

Your breath !

What flower do you have to keep a look
out for in the garden ?

Anenome !

Why did the man jump up and down
after taking his medicine ?

Because he forgot to shake the bottle
before he took it !

Which famous artist had a bad cold?

Vincent van Cough!

Why did the burglar buy a surf board?

He wanted to start a crime wave!

What does a toad sit on ?

A toadstool !

What does a toad use for making furniture ?

A toad's tool !

Why don't pigs telephone one another ?

Because there is too much crackling on the line !

Why are pigs no good at do-it-yourself ?

Because they are ham-fisted !

Why did the burglar break into
the music shop ?

He was after the lute !

Why did the burglar break into the bakery ?

He wanted to steal the dough !

Why did the burglar go to the bank?

To recycle his bottles!

How do you make a fool laugh on Saturday?

Tell him a joke on Wednesday!

Why must you never make a noise in a hospital?

Because you don't want to wake the sleeping pills!

What is a squirrel's favourite chocolate?

Whole nut!

Where would you find a bee ?

At the start of the alphabet !

Where is there always a queue ?

In between P and R !

What does it mean if your nose starts to run ?

It's trying to catch a cold !

What sort of wine do skeletons like ?

One with plenty of body in it !

How do you make a Venetian blind ?

Paint his spectacles black when he's asleep !

Who is a caveman's favourite band ?

The Stones !

Mary had a little fox,
it ate her little goat,
now everywhere that Mary goes,
she wears her fox-skin coat !

Why does a giraffe have such a long neck ?

Have you ever smelled a giraffe's feet ?!

★

What jungle animal would you find at the North Pole ?

A lost one !

★

What sort of frog is covered in dots and dashes ?

A morse toad !

What does a polar bear use to keep his head warm ?

A polar ice cap !

★

What does a hard of hearing apple have in its ear ?

A lemonade !

★

What do you need to electrocute
an orchestra ?

A good conductor !

What question can you never answer "yes" to ?

"Are you asleep ?!"

★

Good morning, Mr Butcher, do you have pigs' feet ?

Certainly, sir !

Well, wear larger shoes and no-one will notice !

★

How do teddies like to ride horses ?

Bear - back !

★

What do teddies take when they are going on holiday ?

Just the bear essentials !

★

What can you catch but not throw ?

A cold !

Who always puts thyme in his soup ?

A clockmender !

Waiter, there's a small worm in my salad !

Oh, dear, I'll tell the chef to send you a large one !

★

What do you give a dog for breakfast ?

Pooched eggs !

Why couldn't the orange call the apple
on the telephone ?

Because the lime was engaged !

Why are those clothes running out of the
sports shop ?

They're jogging suits !

Why do cows lie down together when it rains ?

To keep each udder dry !

Did you hear about the punk who fell over and
50 others fell over at the same time ?

He started a chain reaction !

What sort of fruit would you find in a diary ?

Dates !

Atissshhhooo! I don't feel very well !

**Wow, I didn't know that having a cold affected
your sense of touch !**

What do vegetarians take home for wages ?

A celery !

What do you call a man who never pays his bills ?

Owen !

What do mice sing at birthday parties ?

For cheese a jolly good fellow !

When should you put your electric guitar in the fridge ?

When you want to play some really cool music !

Which is the greenest city in Europe ?

Brussels !

Which Italian city is good for wandering round?

Rome!

★

Which French city has the best stock of paper?

Rheims!

★

Why are bearded men fearless?

Because they never have a close shave!

What song do sweets sing at parties ?

For he's a jelly good fellow !

How do you write a essay on a giraffe ?

With a long ladder !

How do you shock people at a tea party ?

Serve current buns !

What goes up and never comes down ?

Your age !

My cellar is full of toadstools!

How do you know they're toadstools?

There's not mushroom in there for anything else!

Why do some fishermen suck their maggots before casting their rods?

So they can wait for a fish to bite with baited breath!

Should I give the dog some of my pie?

Certainly not, he didn't want it when I gave it to him earlier!

What sort of ghosts haunt hospitals?

Surgical spirits!

What did the doctor give Cleopatra for her headache ?

An asp - irin !

What do you give a ghost with a headache ?

AAAAGGGGHHHHspirin !

Where do vampires go on holiday ?

Veinice !
How do you know if a bicycle is haunted ?

Look for spooks in the wheels !

What do you get if you cross a skunk with an owl ?

Something that stinks but doesn't give a hoot !

What do you call a doctor with a bright
green stethoscope ?

Doctor !

What sort of parties do vampires like best ?

Fang - cy dress parties !

How do you talk to a hen ?

By using fowl language !

Who is the patron saint of toys ?

Saint Francis of a see-saw !

Why should you never tell your secrets to a piglet ?

Because they might squeal !

★

Which teacher won't allow sick notes ?

The music teacher !

How did the skeleton know it was
going to rain ?

He could feel it in his bones !

What did Frankenstein's monster say when
he was struck by lightning?

"Great! That was *just* what I needed !"

Why did the skeleton go to hospital ?

To have his ghoul stones removed !

What is a juggernaut?

An empty jug!

★

What does B.C. stand for?

Before Calculators!

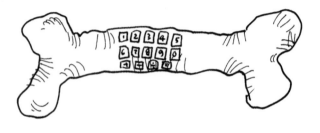

★

What gets wetter the more it dries?

A towel!

★

What did the stupid fencing team take to the Olympics?

5,000 litres of varnish!

What should you do if you find yourself in the
same room as Frankenstein, Dracula, a werewolf,
a vampire and a coven of witches?

**Keep your fingers crossed that it's a
fancy dress party!**

What did one of Frankenstein's ears say
to the other?

I didn't know we lived on the same block!

Which trees grow at the seaside ?

Beech trees !

★

How do you make a Mexican chilli ?

Take him to Iceland !

What do cannibals do at a wedding ?

They toast the bride and groom !

What is a mistake ?

An unmarried female bank robber !

Why is the bookshop
the tallest building in
the town ?

**Because it has the
most stories !**

Who do you ask to see
if you find a twig in
your salad ?

The branch manager !

What sort of person gets paid to make faces all day ?

A clockmaker !

What happened when the vampire went insane ?

He went batty !

★

What sort of tree grows near a volcano ?

A lava tree !

What did the skunk say when the wind
changed direction?

It's all coming back to me now!

★

Why must you always have holes in your socks?

**You wouldn't be able to get your feet
in them if you didn't!**

★

What is yellow, wears glasses and sings?

'Nana Mouskouri!

In which battle was Alexander
the Great killed?

His last one!

In which film does fruit rule the world?

Planet of the Grapes!

Where do squirrels keep their nuts?

In a pan-tree!

Which are the strongest days of the week?

**Saturday and Sunday - all the others
are weak days!**

What is the greatest worldwide use
of cowhide?

To hold cows together!

What do you call someone who can't
stop stealing carpets?

A rug addict!

Why don't mussels share?

They're shellfish!

What kind of room has no doors or windows?

A mushroom!

Which of these is correct -
"egg yolk is white"
"egg yolk are white"

Neither - egg yolk is yellow !

Where would you find a rubber trumpet ?

In an elastic band !

What do you call a lion with no eyes ?

Lon !

Why did the satsuma go to the doctor ?

It wasn't peeling too well !

Where do insects go to dance ?

A cricket ball !

Why are cars rubbish at soccer?

They only have one boot!

★

What do you call a very old vampire?

A gran - pire!

★

What animal uses a nutcracker?

A toothless squirrel!

What music does King Neptune like ?

Sole !

★

What did the doctor say to the woman with a
sausage in each ear, an egg on her head and a
chip up each nostril ?

"You obviously aren't eating properly !"

★

What has no legs but can run across the
bathroom floor ?

Water !

Why is a bad bank like a lazy schoolboy ?

They both lose interest quickly !

What do you throw for a stick insect to fetch ?

A dog !

How do you measure the size of fruit ?

With a green gauge !

★

Why was 10 scared ?

Because 7 8 9 (7 ate 9) !

What runs all the way round a house without moving ?

A fence !

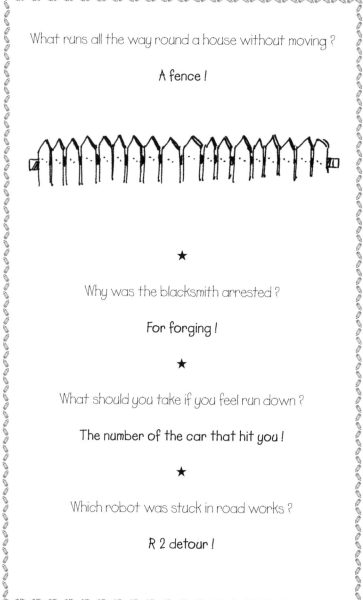

Why was the blacksmith arrested ?

For forging !

What should you take if you feel run down ?

The number of the car that hit you !

Which robot was stuck in road works ?

R 2 detour !

How do hens dance ?

Chick to chick !

Where do Martians live ?

In greenhouses !

What is it called when a fish tells lies in a courtroom ?

Perchery !

What do you give the man who has everything ?

Nothing !

What goes up and down without moving ?

The temperature !

★

Why do woodworm have no friends ?

Because they are boring creatures !

Who drives her children to school in a small car ?

A minimum !

What do vampires do before driving a car ?

They check the wing mirrors !

Why do vampires never marry ?

They are bat - chelors !

★

Where can you go for a quick break by the beach ?

A seaside karate club !

★

What is the best thing to put in a sandwich ?

Your teeth !

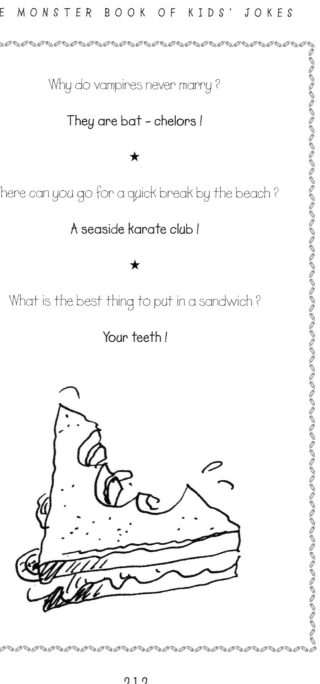

Who writes joke books in *Never Never Land*?

Peter Pun!

How do you stop your nose from running?

Take away its running shoes!

What do you get if you cut
a comedian in two?

A half wit!

What do you get if you
cross a bee with an ape?

Sting Kong!

How do jockeys send
messages to each other?

By horse code!

Why did the cow look into the crystal ball ?

To see if there was a message from the udder side !

Why did the lemon cross the road ?

Because he wanted to play squash !

What do you have to break before you can use it ?

An egg !

Why couldn't the astronauts land on the moon?

Because it was full!

What is worse than a hungry vampire?

A thirsty vampire!

★

Who thought up the series 'Star Trek'?

Some bright Spock!

How can you cook turkey that really tickles the taste buds?

Leave the feathers on!

★

What's the special offer at the pet shop this week?

Buy one cat, get one flea!

FREE

★

What do you call a bike that bites your bottom when you try to get on it?

A vicious cycle!

How do skeletons call their friends ?

On the telebone !

Why did the skeleton pupil stay late at school ?

He was boning up for his exams !

George turns off the light in his bedroom.
The light switch is five metres from the bed,
but he manages to get into his bed before it
is dark. How does he do it ?

He goes to bed in daylight !

What can you only keep once you have given it ?

A promise !

Why did the skeleton run up a tree ?

Because a dog was after his bones !

Why do demons and ghouls get on so
well together ?

Because demons are a ghoul's best friend !

What happened to the boat that sank in
the sea full of piranha fish ?

It came back with a skeleton crew !

Where would you keep sheep covered in ink ?

In a pen !

Why are lots of famous artists French ?

Because they were born in France !

What do you get if you cross a cocker spaniel,
a poodle and a rooster ?

Cockerpoodledoo !

What does a dog get when it finishes
obedience school ?

A pet degree !

Where is the ocean deepest ?

At the bottom !

What goes up and down stairs without moving?

Carpet !

What did the barman say when the ghost
asked for a whisky ?

I'm sorry Sir, we don't serve spirits here !

★

What do you call a skeleton snake ?

A rattler !

How do you join the Dracula fan club ?

Send your name, address and blood group !

What did the skeleton say to his girlfriend?

I love every bone in your body!

★

What's a skeleton's favourite musical instrument?

A trom - bone!

★

What can travel around the world but stays in one corner?

A postage stamp!

★

What flavour ice cream does Dracula like best?

Veinilla!

★

Why do dogs bury bones in the ground?

Where else can you bury them?

What kind of noise annoys an oyster ?

A noisy noise annoys an oyster !

What do you get when you cross a chicken
with a duck ?

A bird that lays down !

What should you do if you find a gorilla
in your bed ?

Sleep somewhere else !

What's a bear's favourite food ?

Tagliateddy !

What does a spider do when he gets angry ?

He goes up the wall !

What time is it when astronauts are hungry ?

Launch time !

★

What is the most slippery country in the world ?

Greece !

★

Where does a general keep his armies ?

Up his sleevies !

★

What kind of fish can't swim ?

Dead ones !

How do you make a submarine sink?

Knock on the door!

What's worse than finding a maggot
in your apple?

Finding half a maggot!

How do you make varnish disappear?

Remove the R!

Why did the chewing gum cross the road?

Because it was stuck to the chicken's foot!

Why did the one-handed man cross
the road?

To get to the second-hand shop!

WHAT DO YOU GET...

What do you get if you cross a toad
with a science fiction film ?

Star Warts !

What do you get if you cross a road
with a blindfold ?

Knocked down !

What do you get if you cross a cow and a camel ?

Lumpy milkshakes !

What do you get if you cross a
bridge with your feet ?

To the other side !

What do you get if you cross a donkey with a mole ?

Mule hills in your garden !

What do you get if you cross a parrot
and a scary film ?

A bad attack of the polly - wobbles !

What do you get if you cross a lawn
and a mattress ?

A flower bed !

What do you get if you cross a car
with a row of mountains ?

A Range Rover

What do you get if you cross a baby and a snake ?

A rattler !

What do you get if you cross a sheep
with a plant?

Cotton wool!

What do you get if you cross a sheep
with a steel bar?

Wire wool!

What do you get if you cross a chicken with
a cemet mixer?

A bricklayer!

What do you get if you cross a mouse
with a tin opener?

**Something that can get the cheese
from the fridge without even
opening the door!**

What do you get if you cross a hive of bees with a jumper knitting pattern?

Nice and swarm!

What do you get if you cross a plant pot and an infant?

A growing child!

What do you get if you cross a fish and a deaf person?

A herring aid!

PARDON...

What do you get if you cross a sheep
with an octopus ?

A jumper with eight arms !

★

What do you get if you cross a dog
with a vegetable ?

A jack brussel terrier !

What do you get if you cross a
comedy author with a ghost ?

A crypt writer !

What do you get if you cross a spinach eater,
a suitmaker and a hippy ?

Popeye the tailor, man !

What do you get if you cross a frog with a cowboy ?

Hoppalong Cassidy !

What do you get if you cross a shark
and Father Christmas ?

Santa Jaws !

What do you get if you cross a spider with a tyre ?

A spinning wheel !

What do you get if you cross a Star Wars
robot with a sheep ?

R 2 D ewe !

What do you get if you cross a waiter
with a slippery floor ?

Flying saucers !

What do you get if you cross a tropical
fruit and a sad dog ?

A melon collie !

What do you get if you cross
a chicken with a kangaroo ?

Pouched eggs !

What do you get if you cross an Irishman with a spider ?

Paddy long legs !

What do you get if you cross a track suit
with a tortoise ?

A shell suit !

What do you get if you cross a cat with a cushion ?

A cat - a - pillow !

What do you get if you cross a canary with a
50-foot long snake ?

A sing - a - long !

What do you get if you cross a glow worm
with a python ?

A 15-foot strip light that can strangle
you to death !

What do you get if you cross a great
invention with a herb ?

A thyme machine !

What do you get if you cross a centipede
with a children's toy ?

A lego, lego, lego, lego, lego, lego,
lego, lego, lego ... set

What do you get if you cross a parking space and a camel?

A camelot!

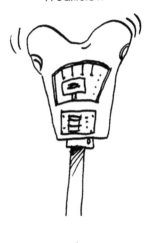

What do you get if you cross an alien with a pair of gloves?

Green fingers!

What do you get if you cross a skeleton and a supermodel?

Not an ounce of fat!

What do you get if you cross a sore throat
and some Christmas decorations?

Tinselitis!

What do you get if you cross a half-open door and
a queue of cars?

A jar of jam!

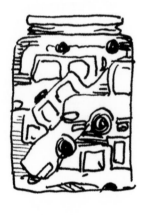

What do you get if you cross a turkey
with an octopus?

A leg for everyone at Christmas dinner!

What do you get if you cross China with a car horn?

Hong King!

What do you get if you cross a worm
and a young goat?

A dirty kid!

What do you get if you cross a bed with
a set of cricket wickets?

A three poster!

What do you get if you cross a hat
with a mountain top?

A peaked cap!

What do you get if you cross Dracula and Al Capone?

A fangster!

What do you get if you cross a rodent and
someone who cleans your home ?

A mousekeeper !

What do you get if you cross a glow worm with a beer ?

Light ale !

What do you get if you cross a surgeon
and an octopus ?

A doctorpus !

What do you get if you cross a robot
with a drinks machine ?

C - tea - P - O !

What do you get if you cross a robot with a foot ?

C - 3 - P - toe !

What do you get if you cross a ghost
and a Christmas play ?

A phantomime !

What do you get if you cross a
vegetable with a 42-kilometre run ?

A marrow - thon !

What do you get if you cross a joke book
with an Oxo cube ?

A laughing stock !

★

What do you get if you cross a golf club
and a burrowing animal ?

A mole in one !

What do you get if you cross a playing card
with a fizzy drink ?

Joker cola !

What do you get if you cross a werewolf
and a frog ?

A creature that can bite you from the
other side of the road !

What do you get if you cross an
octopus with a fountain pen ?

A squidgy pen with 8 nibs that
makes all its own ink !

What athlete do you get if you cross
a snake and a sheep ?

A long jumper !

What do you get if you cross a television
personality and a jungle animal?

A gnus reader!

What do you get if you cross a glow worm
with a ham salad?

A light meal!

What do you get if you cross a vampire
with the middle of the week?

Winceday!

What do you get if you cross vampires
with some cheddar ?

Bancheese !

What do you get if you cross a horse with a
cake and a long rubber strip ?

A bun - gee - gee jumper !

What do you get if you cross a ghost with a
Spanish holiday resort ?

The Ghosta Brava !

What do you get if you cross a camel and a ghost ?

Something that goes hump in the night !

What do you get if you cross a butcher and a dance ?

A meatball !

What do you get if you cross a
worm with an elephant ?

Great big holes in your garden !

What do you get if you cross a cat with a lemon ?

A sour puss !

What do you get if you cross a
ghost with a chicken ?

A poultry - geist !

What do you get if you cross a monster with a pig ?

Frankenswine !

What do you get if you cross a
day of the week with bubble gum ?

Chewsday !

What do you get if you cross an ant and a calculator ?

An account - ant !

What do you get if you cross a
vampire and a teacher ?

Lots of blood tests !

What do you get if you cross a skeleton
with some crockery ?

Bone china !

What do you get if you cross a skeleton
with a Scottish prince ?

Boney Prince Charlie !

What do you get if you cross a fairy and a turkey ?

A very strange goblin !

What do you get if you cross a cricket ball and an alien ?

A bowling green !

What do you get if you cross a joke book
and two dozen eggs ?

A book with at least 24 yolks in it !

What do you get if you cross a hairdresser
and a werewolf ?

A creature with an all-over perm !

What do you get if you cross milk, fruit
and a scary film ?

A strawberry milk shake !

★

What do you get if you cross a pig and an old radio ?

Lots of crackling !

What do you get if you cross an army
and some babies ?

The infantry !

What do you get if you cross a mountain
with hiccups ?

A volcano !

What do you get if you cross a vampire with a dog ?

A bloodhound !

What do you get if you cross a tall
building and a home for pigs ?

A sty - scraper !

What do you get if you cross a bun
and a cattle rustler ?

A beef burglar !

What do you get if you cross a window
and a shirt collar ?

A pane in the neck !

What do you get if you cross the sea with a pot of chilli ?

A Mexican wave !

What do you get if you cross a
can of oil and a mouse ?

I don't know, but at least it doesn't squeak !

★

What do you get if you cross a sheep
with a discount store ?

Lots of baaaaagains !

What do you get if you cross a holidaymaker
and an elephant ?

Something that carries its own trunk !

★

What do you get if you cross a ghost
and a pair of glasses ?

Spook - tacles !

What do you get if you cross a feather
with a carnation ?

Tickled pink !

What do you get if you cross a boy band
and some bottles of lemonade ?

A pop group !

What do you get if you cross an ape with an oven ?

A hairy griller !

What do you get if you cross a toad with
someone who tells strange jokes ?

Someone with a wart sense of humour !

What do you get if you cross a fish and a birdcage ?

A perch !

What do you get if you cross a
jeweller's shop with a boxer ?

A window full of boxing rings !

★

What do you get if you cross an oil well
with bad manners ?

Crude oil !

What do you get if you cross a skunk
and a winning lottery ticket ?

Stinking rich !

What do you get if you cross a donkey and
a three-legged milking stool ?

A wonkey !

What do you get if you cross a
cat with a set of watercolours ?

Pusster paints !

What do you get if you cross a dog and an elephant ?

No more post !

What do you get if you cross a giraffe and a dog ?

Something that bites the tyres of low flying aircraft !

What do you get if you cross a crying baby
and a football fan?

A footbawler!

What do you get if you cross a ball
and a blunt instrument?

A football club!

What do you get if you cross poison ivy with
a four-leaf clover ?

A rash of good luck !

What do you get if you cross a sheep
and an ink cartridge ?

**Something that only a sheepdog can
get into a pen !**

What do you get if you cross a golden retriever
with a tortoise ?

**An animal that goes to the newsagent's and
comes back with last week's newspaper !**

What do you get when you cross a vampire
with a computer ?

**A know-it-all that's really a
pain in the neck !**

What do you get if you cross electricity
and a chicken ?

Battery eggs !

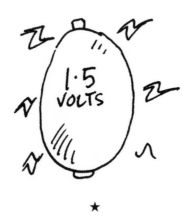

What do you get if you cross a
pencil with window covers ?

Blinds that draw themselves !

What do you get if you cross a
Welshman and a saint ?

Good Evans !

What do you get if you cross a
budgie and a clown?

Something that's cheep and cheerful!

What do you get if you cross a comedian, an owl and a
tube of adhesive?

A wit who glues!

What do you get if you steal part of an elderly
Scotsman's fish supper?

A chip off the old Jock!

What do you get if you cross a scratch
on your arm and a fruit ?

A lemon sore - bit !

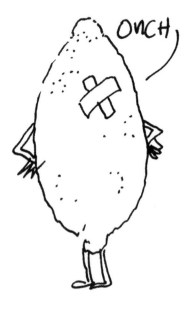

★

What do you get if you cross a
rhinoceros with a cat ?

Very worried mice !

What do you get if you cross a
cartoon with some bubble gum ?

A carica - chewer !

What do you get if you cross a sheep with a pub ?

A cocktail baaa !

What do you get if you cross a dinosaur
with a witch ?

Tyrannosaurus hex !

What do you get if you cross a
field of cows and a motor boat ?

Pat pat pat pat pat pat pat pat pat... !

What do you get if you cross a flea with a rabbit ?

Bugs Bunny !

259

What do you get if you cross a range of mountains
with a dancer ?

Something huge dancing peak to peak !

What do you get if you cross a witch
and an iceberg ?

A cold spell !

What do you get if you cross a baby with a UFO ?

An unidentified crying object !

What do you get if you cross an octopus with a cow ?

An animal that can milk itself !

What do you get if you cross an alligator with a flower ?

I don't know, but I'm not going to smell it !

AWFUL ALPHABET

ALLOCATE

Allocate

Say hello to Kate !

A

Abandon   When a pop group is playing !

Abrade   A Chinese knife !

Accident   When you cut yourself chopping firewood !

Address   Something a woman wears at her wedding !

Adorn   A beautiful start to the day !

Aftermath   The result of a catastrophe -
it's where we get the word 'maths'!

Airliner   The person who paints the lines down the
side of jumbo jets!

Allocate   Say hello to Kate!

Antelope   When two ants run off to get married!

Antifreeze   When your mum's sister goes out
without a coat in winter !

Arrest   What a burglar gets when he goes to bed !

Automate   A robot for a best pal !

B

Bacteria   The rear entrance to a cafeteria!

Bandage   The average age of a pop group!

Banshee   Don't let that ghost in here!

Barber   Sheep trained as a hairdresser!

Bark   The sound made by a wooden dog!

Bateau   What the French used when they played tenniso, squasho and cricketo!

Batman   The secret identity of Dracula !

Beauty spot   When flowers grow out of your head !

Berth   Where they keep any babies born at sea !

Beverage   Slightly worse than average !

Beware   What bees wear, of course !

Bichromate   A friend you go cycling with !

C

Cabbage   How old a taxi is !

Cagoule   Ghost who goes around in a car !

Canary Islands   Where cats like to go for their holidays !

Candidate   The sweets you take to impress a new girlfriend !

Capacity   The size of your head !

Carousel   A used car dealership !

Carrot   Rust !

Chemistry   The tree you end up in when the lab
             explodes !

Chipmunk   Chef in a monastery !

Clay pigeon   School dinners !

Crime Wave   Where robbers go to surf !

Czech   Money paid into a foreign bank account !

D

Debate   De thing on de fish hook !

Defeatist   Someone who designs shoes !

Demijohn   Robin Hood's best friend !

Dentist   Car body repairer !

Descant   Ant that lives in a school !

Desert   Pudding made from sand!

Detention   The fear of being kept behind at school!

Diplomat   A mat for kneeling on when you meet a VIP!

Discount   How much a shop assistant will knock off a new CD player 'cos he's no good at maths!

Distressed   Having all your hair cut off!

Dynamo   Welshman refusing to cut the grass!

E

Earring	Answer the telephone !
Eclipse	Hedge cutter !
Editor	Policeman's truncheon !
Eider	Not bothered !

Einstein	One glass of beer !

Elastic band   A group who play rubber instruments!

Electrocute   Pretty electrician!

Engineers   Ears on an engine!

Extension   More stress caused by a longer exam!

F

Factory   The place where they make trees !

Falter   Give a girl low marks in a test !

Fax   The truth !

Feedback   A baby being sick !

Fez   Nickname for a pheasant !

Fiddlesticks   Violin bows !

Figurehead   Someone who is good at maths !

Finishing school   The start of the summer holidays !

Fish and chips   What they serve in the canteen of a nuclear power station !

Flash bulb   A light bulb that thinks very highly of itself !

Footnote   When you try to hide a bank note with your shoe, until no-one is looking and you can pick it up !

Frankinsence   The man who runs the perfume shop !

G

Gamekeeper   The teacher who confiscates your Nintendo!

Gazette   Baby gazelle!

Germinate   Bacteria in bad food!

Genealogy   Finding out if there is a genie in your family history!

Glacier   The cold stare of the man fixing the windows you smashed!

Gymkhana   The owner of the local riding school!

H

Hail stones   Over-cooked water droplets !

Hallmarks   Black skid marks in the corridor, which you make as you screech to a halt when a teacher suddenly comes round the corner !

Handiwork   A job just around the corner from where you live !

Hatchback   A car full of baby chicks !

Headrest   Lunch time !

Heirloom   When someone leaves you a pet rabbit in their will !

Hemlock   Special stitch used around the bottom of a skirt !

Highway code   What hitch hikers catch from standing about in the rain !

277

Hippodrome   Where hippos go to learn to fly !

Honeycomb   What bees use to style their hair !

Hot Cross Bun What you get if you pour boiling
               water down a rabbit hole !

I

Icicle   A bicycle with a bit missing !

Ideogram   Telegram sent to an idiot !

Ignite   Eskimo's bedtime !

Impatient   Someone fidgeting in the doctor's
                      waiting room !

Implicate   Blame Kate for something she didn't do !

Infant   Baby elephant !

Infantry   Army made up of baby elephants !

Infiltrate   Sneaking Phil into the football match without paying !

Instep   The latest dance !

Instrumental   Driven crazy by next door's piano lessons !

J

Jackdaw   Small entrance for birds found in a tree !

Jam-packed   A very full sandwich !

Jargon   Stolen jar !

Jitterbug   Insect that can't sit still !

Joan of Arc   Noah's wife !

Jodhpurs   Trousers worn by a cat !

Juggernaut   Empty jug !

K

Kaleidoscope Bump into people while you're looking through a telescope !

Ketchup Run as fast as a bottle of tomato sauce !

Kettle drum What the orchestra uses to make a cup of tea !

Kipper Sleeping fish !

Knickers Burglars !

Knitwear Jumper for a fool !

L

Labrador   Dog that helps a scientist with his experiments!

Lacewing   Where prisoners make lace!

Lactose   Monster with the ends of his feet cut off!

Lambda   Greek letter invented by a sheep!

Lamination   Country ruled by sheep!

Lassitude   Monster eats girl!

Launderette   A small launder – but I've no idea what a launder is!

Leek   Vegetable that is not allowed on a boat!

Lemonade   What you give a deaf orange!

Leopard Lily   A plant you should never sniff!

Level-headed   What you will be if someone drops a car on your head !

Lie detector   What sneaky teachers use to see who is asleep in the class !

Light-fingered   Someone who steals bulbs !

Lockjaw   What you are likely to get if you swallow a bunch of keys !

Logarithm   Music played by pieces of wood !

Loose leaf   Where to store all the fallen autumn
folder   leaves !

Lukewarm   What Luke is every winter because he
                    manages to sit next to the only
                    radiator in the class room !

Luminous   Toilets that glow in the dark !

M

Macintosh   Waterproof computer !

Magician   Anyone who can score more than 14% in a maths examination !

Magneto   Italian for 'magnet' !

Mammoth   Large hairy moth with tusks - now extinct !

Manure What some odd people put on their rhubarb – I prefer custard on mine !

Marionette Marion's little sister !

Marksman Teacher with exam results file !

Marxist Someone who watches old Marx Brothers films all day !

Melancholy What you get if you cross a sheep dog with a fruit !

Mental block   When someone stands in front of the
door in the exam room to stop you
escaping !

Metacarpus   Scene of an accident involving a
motor vehicle and a cat !

Metronome   Short person working on the Paris
underground railway system !

Minimum   Metronome's mother !

Mumbo jumbo   Elephant who doesn't speak clearly !

MUMBLE...
MUTTER...

Mushroom   The room where all the Eskimos go to train their husky dogs to pull sleds. You will often hear the word 'mush' as you walk past !

Mute   A lute without any strings !

N

Nag   Tell off a horse !

Nappy   Liable to fall asleep in history lessons !

Negligent   Man in a nightie !

Newsagent   Spy hiding behind a newspaper !

Nickname   Put someone else's name on your exam paper !

Nightmare   Horse that can only be ridden during the hours of darkness !

Nipper   Baby crab !

Nose Cone   Trip up and splat the end of your ice cream into your face !

Nuclear fuel   Someone who messes around in a power station !

O

Oblique   The feeling you get at the start of a
three-hour maths exam!

Oblong   The feeling you get when you have finished
all the questions and it is still only halfway
through a three-hour maths exam!

Octangle   The feeling an octopus gets in a three-hour
maths exam!

Offenbach   Noisy dog!

Offensive   Garden fence that nobody likes!

Opt out   Leave the sports field because of a
                damaged foot !

Orchid   Baby orchestra !

Orienteering   Trying to find your way to Asia with
                    out a map or compass !

Outcrop   That little tuft of hair that the barber
                    always seems to miss !

Outnumber   Finally leaving that three-hour
                    maths exam !

P

Padlocks   Handcuffs for cats and dogs !

Pamphlet   Leaflet written by Pam !

Pant   Half a pair of trousers !

Paranoid   Robot who is convinced that someone is out to get him !

Parasite   Where leeches go on their summer holiday !

Parking meter   Space for a very, very short car!

Parrot fashion   What trendy parrots wear!

Part exchange   Transplant surgery!

Party wall   What neighbours bang on when you make too much noise!

Pas de deux   Less than 2% in the French exam!

Picket   What you do when your nose goes on strike!

Pigment   Special paint for colouring pigs!

Q

Quadrangle Fight in the school playground !

Quadratic equation Maths problem that you need at least 4 people to solve !

Quasimodo Don't remember the name, but the face rings a bell !

Quicksilver Easily spent pocket money !

R

Racquet   Noise made by tennis players!

Rainbow   What the rain wears in its hair!

Ransom   Only completed part of the school
                cross-country race!

Ransom note A letter that someone gives the
                 teacher to tell him that you only ran
                 part of the cross-country!

Ratbag   Mouse's rucksack !

Ray gun   Former President of the United States !

Recycle   Do up an old bike !

Rehearse   Drive back to the graveyard !

Remainder   All the numbers you are left with at the end of the maths exam !

Reverse charge   Who you telephone to stop a herd of wild elephants !

Roller skate   Sea fish with his own wheels !

Rosette   Small rose !

Royal blue   When the Queen is fed up !

Rubber tree   What the use to make those pencils with an eraser at the end !

Rustle   Paper boy !

S

Salad dressing   What you will see salad do when it gets up in the morning !

Sand Bank   Where camels keep their savings !

Satire   Sitting in a tall chair !

Scatter cushions   Result of a pillow fight !

Scholastic   What holds up your P.E. shorts !

Schumacher   Cobbler !

Scissors   Swimming leg action designed to cut through the water !

Scotch egg   What you get if you feed chickens whisky !

Scrunch   Lunchbox run over by a bus !

Sea horse   What the idiot bought because he wanted to play water polo !?

Semiconductor   Part-time bus driver !

Shamrock   A plant pretending to be a stone!

Sheba   Queen with a lot of sheep!

Sheep dip   What wolves have at parties!

Sheep dog trial   What happens after sheep dogs are arrested!

Sheet lightning   What happens if lightning hits your bed!

Shellfish   Crustaceans that never share anything!

Shingle   How a drunk asks for one !

Shortbread   A loaf cut in half !

Spell checker   Computer software for witches !

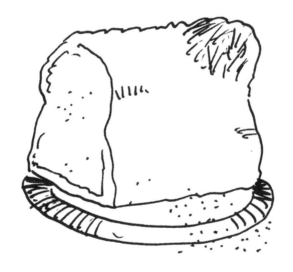

T

Tactical   Tickling a small nail !

Tap dancer   Someone trying to do the River Dance in the sink !

Telethon   Well, thwitch it off then thilly !

Tinfoil   Not very thick foil !

Tirade   Robbery in a tie shop !

Toadstool   Hammer belonging to a toad !

Toulouse   Two toilets !

Track suit   What a railway line wears when it goes out jogging !

Traffic jam   What policemen have in their sandwiches !

Tycoon   Someone who has made a lot of money selling ties !

U

Ultimatum   When you tell your friend for the last time !

Umpire   Vampire who can't spell !

Unaware   Boxer shorts !

Undecided   Not knowing what colour unaware to put on !

Underpass   Handing secret notes under your desk !

Underrate   Any number from 1 to 7 !

Unit   Fool !

University   Training school for poets !

Unleaded   Empty pencil case !

Unstable   Horse that lives in a field !

V

Vacuum cleaner Used to keep outer space nice and tidy !

Vampire Where you go to hire a vamp !

Varnish A posh way of disappearing !

Vespers Very quiet whispers !

Vest Opposite to East !

W

Waistcoat　　Jacket made from scraps of material !

Wardrobe　　Cupboard that joins the army !

Warhead　　Head teacher who joins the army !
　　　　　　　Hurrah !

Warren　　A man who keeps pet rabbits !

Weight watcher　Someone who spends a lot of time
　　　　　　　looking at their tummy !

X - Y - Z

X-Ray   Used to belong to Ray !

Xylophone   What aliens from the planet Xylo use to telephone each other !

Yak   What you say when you stand in something nasty !

Yam   How they say Jam in Holland !

Yardstick   Sweeping brush with a missing head !

Yellowhammer What you shout when you hit your thumb !

Yellow Pages Homework book with tea spilled on it !

Yoga Cartoon bear !

Yokel Farmworker who paints egg yolks yellow !

Zebra Mobile road crossing !

Zermatt   What you wipe zer feet on !

Zinc   Where you wash your hands !

Zing   What you do with zongs in a choir !

Zoo   What a solicitor does !

Zoom lens   The sound of a camera falling from a great height !

Zulu   The toilets in the zoo !

HOSPITAL HOWLERS

Doctor, doctor, my son is turning into a
cricket bat !

Well, this has got me stumped !

Why did the angry doctor have to retire?

Because he had lost all his patients!

Doctor, doctor, I think I've got an inferiority complex!

No you haven't – you really are terrible at everything!

Ah, Mr Smith, have your eyes ever been checked?

No doctor, they've always been blue!

Doctor, doctor, there's a man to see you with a wooden leg called Jenkins.

What's his other leg called?

★

Doctor, doctor, I think I'm turning into a wasp!

Hmm, give me a buzz if things get really bad!

★

Doctor, doctor, I've just been stung by a wasp!

Did you put anything on it?

No, he seemed to enjoy it just as it was!

Doctor, doctor, I've got an itchy, spotty patch on my nose. Should I put cream on it?

Now, now, let's not do anything rash!

Doctor, doctor, I've not stopped laughing since my operation!

Well, I told you the surgeon would have you in stitches!

Doctor, doctor, I've got pigeon toes!

Don't worry we'll find a suitable tweetment for you... but for now just put this bird seed in your shoes!

Doctor, doctor, my belly is so big I'm embarrassed by it !

Have you try to diet ?

Yes, but whatever colour I use it still sticks out !

★

Doctor's Bookshelf...

TRAINING TO BE A SURGEON

by

I. CUTTEM - OPEN

Doctor, doctor, I can't stop shoplifting !

Try taking two of these pills every morning,
and if that doesn't work, bring me a CD player
next week !

Doctor, doctor, thank you for coming – I'm at
death's door !

Don't worry, I'll pull you through !

Doctor, doctor, is it true that you can get pills to
improve your memory ?

Of course you can, how many would you like ?

How many what ?

Which king was also a doctor ?

William the corn curer !

Did you hear about the appendix who went out and bought a new suit - he heard that the doctor was going to take him out !

Which kings needed medical attention ?

Charles the sick and Henry the ache !

Doctor, doctor, what can I do to help me get to sleep ?

Have you tried counting sheep ?

Yes, but then I have to wake up to drive home again !

Doctor, doctor, I've got a terrible cough !

Well you should practice more !

Doctor, doctor, I feel like a goat !

Really – and how are the kids ?

Doctor, doctor, I think I'm turning into a fish !

Well, just hop up onto the scales !

Doctor, doctor, After the operation on my hand will I be able to play the piano ?

Of course you will Mr Smith !

Great - because I never could before !

Doctor, doctor, I think I'm turning into a bridge !

Really - what's come over you ?

Doctor, doctor, those tablets you gave me last week seem to get smaller every day !

Yes, they're slimming pills !

Doctor, doctor, I think I'm turning into a toad !

Don't worry, we can do a hoperation for that these days !

Doctor, doctor, can you put me in touch with the local plastic surgeon ?

I'm afraid not, he sat too close to the radiator last night and melted !

Doctor, doctor, I have a fish hook stuck in the side of my mouth !

I thought you were waiting to see me with baited breath !

Doctor, doctor, I've just been stung by a giant wasp!

I'll give you some cream to put on it!

Don't be silly - it'll be miles away by now!

Doctor, doctor, my new job at the laundrette is very tiring!

I thought you looked washed out!

Doctor, doctor, I got trampled by a load of cows!

So I herd!

Doctor, doctor, I get a lot of headaches from my wooden leg.

Why is that ?

Because my wife keeps hitting me over the head with it !

Doctor, doctor, my snoring wakes me up every night !

Try sleeping in another bedroom, then you won't be able to hear it !

Doctor, doctor, I keep imagining I'm a sunken ship and it's really got me worried!

Sounds to me like you're a nervous wreck!

Doctor, doctor, I think I have a split personality!

I'd better give you a second opinion then!

Doctor, doctor, I feel quite like my old self again!

Oh dear, I better put you back on the tablets then!

Doctor, doctor, I'm having trouble with my breathing.

I'll give you something that will soon put a stop to that!

Doctor, doctor, I'm going to die in 51 seconds!

I'll be with you in a minute!

Doctor, doctor, what can you give me for my kidneys ?

How about a pound of onions ?

Doctor, doctor, I've fractured my elbow bone !

Humerus ?

Well, I don't think it's particularly funny !

Doctor, doctor, is this disease contagious ?

Not at all !

Then why are you standing out on the window ledge ?

Doctor, doctor, you don't really think I'm turning into a grandfather clock do you ?

No, I was just winding you up !

Doctor, doctor, I keep thinking I'm a big bar of chocolate!

Come and sit here, and don't worry, I won't bite – I'm just a big old pussycat really!

★

Doctor, doctor, I think I've broken my neck!

Don't worry – keep your chin up!

Doctor, doctor, I feel like a dog!

Sit down!

Doctor, doctor, what did the x-ray of my head show ?

Absolutely nothing !

Doctor, doctor, you've got to help me - I just can't stop my hands shaking !

Do you drink a lot ?

Not really - I spill most of it !

Doctor, doctor, I think I have acute appendicitis !

Yes, it is rather nice isn't it ?

Doctor, doctor, I think I'm a telephone.

Well, take these pills and if they don't work give me a ring !

GRIM GIGGLES

What do you call an overweight vampire ?

Draculard !

How many skeletons can you fit in an empty coffin?

Just one - after that it's not empty any more!

What did the mummy ghost say to the little ghost?

Don't spook until you're spooken to!

Where would you find a suitable gift for
a tortured ghost?

In a chain store!

What kind of yogurt do vampires like best?

Necktarine flavour!

Why did the vampire bite a computer?

He wanted to get onto the interneck!

What day of the week do vampires and werewolves like best?

Moonday - especially full-moonday!

What sort of monster would you find up your nose?

A bogeyman!

How do you know if there is a ghost in a hotel ?

Ask to see the hotel in - spectre !

★

Why should you never run if you see a werewolf ?

Because they love fast food !

★

How do mummies go into their pyramids ?

Gift-wrapped !

How do you get a *mummy* interested in music ?

Play him some wrap !

★

What should you never order if you're eating out
with a vampire ?

Steak and chips !

★

What is a ghost's favourite animal ?

The whale !

Why do ghosts go back to the same place
every year for their holidays ?

They like their old haunts best !

Vampire hunter's menu. . .

GARLIC BREAD

followed by

HAMMERED STEAK

and finally

HOT CROSS BUNS

What do you call a ghost that
doesn't scare anyone ?

A failure !

What does a well brought up vampire say
after he has bitten your neck?

Fang you very much!

VAMPIRE SAYINGS...

Once bitten - twice bitten!

A neck in your hand is worth two in a bush!

A stitch in time - means I can come
back for some more!

There's many a slip twixt neck and lip!

What does a skeleton feed his dog?

Anything but bones!

Why was the cannibal looking peaky?

He had just eaten a Chinese dog!

Why do skeletons take a dog with them to the seaside ?

They need something to bury them in the sand !

Why do skeletons drink lots of milk ?

Because calcium is good for your bones !

★

What do skeletons eat on Good Friday ?

Hot cross bones !

Why do skeletons dislike horror films ?

Because they scare them to the marrow !

★

What sort of jokes do skeletons enjoy ?

Rib ticklers !

★

What do skeletons
sing at birthday
parties ?

**"Femur jolly good
fellow..."**

★

Why was the
skeleton's jacket
in shreds ?

**Because he had
very sharp
shoulder blades !**

What do skeleton schoolchildren wear ?

Knee caps !

What do vampires eat at parties ?

Fang - furters !

How do vampires and ghosts go on holiday ?

By scareplane !

What did the teacher say to the naughty
vampires in class ?

Stop Dracularking about !

Why did the cannibal live on his own ?

He was fed up with other people !

Did you hear about the ghost who cut down trees at three o'clock in the morning?

He liked to make a stump in the night!

What do you call twin ghosts?

Dead ringers!

Why was the vampire lying dead on the floor of the restaurant?

It was a steak house!

What does a young boy ghost do to get a girlfriend?

He woooooooos her!

What are the only jobs that skeletons can get?

As skeleton staff!

Did you hear about the two ghosts
who got married?

It was love at first fright!

What do ghosts do if they are afraid?

Hide under a sheet!

★

What is the difference between a ghost
and a biscuit?

Have you tried dipping a ghost in your tea?

How does a skeleton know when it's going to rain ?

He just gets a feeling in his bones !

Where do vampires get washed ?

In the bat room !

What room must all werewolf homes have ?

A changing room !

GHASTLY GHOSTLY SAYINGS...

Two's company - three's a shroud !

Never kick a ghost while he's down -
your foot will go straight through him !

He who laughs last - obviously hasn't
seen the ghost standing behind him !

Why did the skull go to the disco on his own ?

He had no body to go with !

What do little ghosts wear when it rains ?

Boo - ts and ghoul - oshes !

★

What do ghosts carry their luggage in
when they go on holiday ?

Body bags !

Why did the ghosts have a party ?

They wanted to lift their spirits !

★

What can you use to flatten a ghost ?

A spirit level !

What do skeletons learn about at school ?

Decimals and fractures !

SKELEMENU...

Ox-tail soup

followed by

Spare ribs and finger buffet

finishing with

Marrowbone jelly and custard !

What do you call a vampire who has been in the pub ?

Drunkula !

★

What do you call a vampire that hides in the kitchen ?

Spatula !

★

What do you call a vampire *mummy* ?

Wrapula !

★

What do you call a young vampire ?

Draculad !

What do you call a vampire that attacks insects?

A cricket bat!

What is evil and ugly on the inside and
green on the outside?

A witch dressed as a cucumber!

Why was the little boy unhappy to win first prize
for the best costume at the Halloween party?

Because he just came to pick up his sister!

What has handles and flies?

A witch in a dustbin!

Why don't cannibals eat weathermen?

Because they give them wind!

What is evil, ugly and bounces ?

A witch on a trampoline !

How did Frankenstein's monster escape from
the police ?

He made a bolt for it !

What sort of music do vampires and ghosts like best ?

Haunted house music !

If a monster buys you a chair for your birthday
should you accept it ?

Yes - but don't let him plug it in !

What happens if you see twin witches ?

You won't be able to tell which witch is which !

MAD MARTIANS

How often do you find toilets in space?

Once in a loo moon!

Why didn't the Martian have his birthday party on the moon?

There was no atmosphere!

What is soft and sweet and fluffy and comes from Mars?

A Mars-mallow!

What do astronauts have in their packed lunch?

Launcheon meat!

How do you know that Saturn is married?

You can see the ring!

When the alien picked up his brand new spaceship he was really pleased - he'd never had a New F O before!

What sort of spaceships do aliens from the planet Footwear use?

Shoe F Os!

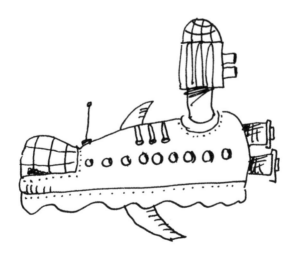

What game do bored aliens play?

Astro - noughts and crosses!

★

How did the space aliens go into the space ark?

R 2 D 2 by R 2 D 2!

★

Why did the spaceship land outside
your bedroom?

You must have left the landing light on!

★

What do you call a space creature that
doesn't pass his space exams?

A fail - ien!

★

What is the smallest space explorer called?

A mouse - tronaut!

What do space ramblers like to do ?

Go on Star Treks !

★

What do you *NEVER* get if you cross a
bug-eyed alien with a dog ?

Burgled !

★

Why are aliens good gardeners ?

They have green fingers !

What robots are made from small planets?

Aster - droids!

Where do aliens keep their sandwiches?

In a launch box!

Knock, knock...
Who's there?
Jupiter.
Jupiter who?
Jupiter space ship on my front lawn?!

What goes in one year and out the other?

A time machine!

If astronauts breathe oxygen during the day,
what do they breathe at night?

Nitrogen!

What is the first thing an alien puts on when he gets out of bed ?

His feet – on the floor !

What is the weakest part of space called ?

The punyverse !

What do you call a vampire version of Star Trek ?

The Necks Generation !

Why was the thirsty alien hanging around the computer ?

He was looking for the space bar !

Where do astronauts leave their spaceships ?

At parking meteors !

Knock, knock...
Who's there ?
Saturn.
Saturn who ?
Saturn front of this spaceship waiting for take-off !

Human - Why have you got holes in your hand ?

Alien - I have been using the computer !

Human - But that's not dangerous !

Alien - Maybe not on Earth, but on my
planet when we talk about computer bytes
we mean something different !

Why do creatures from the planet Thaaarrrgh wear
slimy green braces ?

To hold up their slimy green trousers !

What do you call a glass robot ?

See through P O !

Why couldn't the moon eat any more dinner?

Because it was full!

What teddy bear story do robot children
read at bedtime?

Tinny the Pooh!

What does the alien hairdresser do when the
shadow of the Earth obscures the Sun?

Eclipse!

What did the grape say when the space monster trod on him?

Nothing - he just let out a little whine!

Why is the letter V like a space monster?

Because it comes after U!

Which part of a spacesuit is German?

The Helmut!

How does the solar system hold up its trousers ?

With an asteroid belt !

Which ancient Egyptian king would you find in space ?

Tutankhamoon !

What holds the moon up ?

Moonbeams !

Why are alien kitchens always such a mess ?

Because of all the flying saucers !

What would you do if you saw a spaceman ?

Park in it, man !

Why did the alien buy a twisted spaceship ?

He wanted to travel at warp speed !

Why couldn't the idiot's spaceship travel
at the speed of light ?

Because he took off in the dark !

What do you call dishonest spaceships ?

Lying saucers !

What sort of spaceships do secret
agents fly in ?

Spying saucers !

What do you call miserable spaceships ?

Sighing saucers !

Which alien has the best hearing ?

The eeriest !

Which space villain looks like a pair of wellies ?

Darth Waders !

What sort of music do space aliens like best ?

Heavy metal !

Where do they lock up naughty space creatures ?

Jailien !

Why does Captain Kirk make the crew clean the
Starship Enterprise ?

He likes things to be Spock and span !

Where do you sometimes hear singing in space ?

When you fly past a pop star !

Why did the alien build a spaceship
from feathers ?

He wanted to travel light years !

**Did you hear about the alien poet? She
wrote universes !**

Why did Captain Kirk shave his head ?

To baldly go where no-one had gone before !

Did you hear about the silly alien who
built a spaceship from herbs ?

He wanted to travel through thyme !

What fast food do computers eat ?

Ram burgers !

What piece of sports equipment does every alien own ?

A tennis rocket !

Why did the alien take a nuclear missile to the party ?

In case he fancied blowing up some balloons !

Why did the boy become an astronaut ?

Because he was no earthly good !

I want to be an astronaut when I grow up !

What high hopes you have !

Did you hear about the man who was captured by
extra-terrestrial teddy bears ?

He had a close encounter of the furred kind !

Why don't aliens celebrate Christmas ?

Because they don't like to give away their presence !

Who is long, slippery, and always phones home
when he goes sightseeing ?

E.T. the extra - tourist - eel !

How does a robot shave ?

With a laser blade !

Did you hear about the overweight alien ?

He had to wear a not – very – much – space – suit!

What do you call a spaceship with a
faulty air-conditioning unit ?

A frying saucer !

If Martians live on Mars and Venusians
live on Venus, who lives on Pluto ?

Fleas !

What are aliens' favourite sweets ?

Martian – mallows !

What did the metric alien say ?

Take me to your litre !

What did the alien say to the garden ?

Take me to your weeder !

What did the tree alien say when he landed on Earth ?

Take me to your cedar !

Why is an alien like a collection of famous
actors' autographs ?

They've both come from the stars !

Did you hear about the alien who flew a spaceship
from Neptune to Uranus in just 3 minutes ?

**He's listed in the Guinness Book Of Out-Of-This-World
Records !**

ODDS AND ENDS

Why are you taking that shovel to your
singing class ?

So I can reach the low notes !

What do you call a an underwater spy ?

James Pond !

What sort of dancing will elephants
do in your front room ?

Break dancing !

Knock, knock...
Who's there ?
Boo.
Boo who ?
No need to get upset, it's just a game !

What time is it when you have
eaten half of your lunch?

Half ate!

Doctor, doctor, I feel like the man in the moon!

What's come over you?

A cow!

★

Why did the woman wear a helmet at the dinner table?

She was on a crash diet!

How do electricians get over high fences ?

They volt !

I asked for vegetarian sausage -
these are made from beef !

But the cow was a vegetarian !

Where does Father Christmas go
for his summer holidays ?

Santa Maria !

Hello Carol, how was your first day at school ?

First? You mean I have to go back again ?!

Did you hear about the cowboy who used to sit up all night making models of cows from tissue paper! He was sacked for rustling !

Why didn't the celebrity hotdog want to be in the movies anymore ?

The rolls weren't good enough !

When do you change the water in a goldfish bowl ?

When they've drunk the first lot !

What do you call a fairy who hasn't had a bath ?

Stinkerbell !

What do ghosts shout at a bad play ?

Boooooooooooo !

★

What do skeletons say after they've seen a really good play ?

"That was a rattling good show !"

★

What do you call a travel agent in the jungle ?

A trip - opotamus !

What drink do Australian bears manufacture ?

Coca - Koala !

Which animal tells the best jokes ?

A stand-up chameleon !

What's the quickest way to get out
of the jungle ?

By ele - copter !

What sort of poetry is known everywhere ?

Uni - verse !

My dad must be the greatest magician ever -
yesterday he turned his car into a side street,
and the day before he turned it into a lay-by !

Waiter - where's my elephant sandwich ?

Sorry Sir, I forgot !

★

What do bogeymen drink ?

Demon - ade !

★

Who do female ghouls get married to ?

Edible bachelors !

★

What prize is awarded each year to the best dieter ?

The No - belly Prize !

Nurse, can you take this patient's temperature please ?

Certainly doctor - where to ?

Why did you give up your job as a fortune teller ?

To be honest I couldn't see any future in it !

Why do boxers like going to parties ?

They love to get to the punch !

What's round, shiny, smelly and comes out at night ?

A foul moon !

Are my indicators working ?

On and off !

How do you know where an escaped train is hiding ?

Just follow the tracks !

What sort of boats do clever school children travel on ?

Scholar - ships !

★

Who runs the bar in the jungle ?

The wine - oceros !

Knock, knock...
Who's there ?
Alison
Alison who ?
Alison to you asking me that question every day !

Knock, knock...
Who's there ?
Alpaca
Alpaca who ?
Alpaca suitcase and leave if you keep
asking these silly questions !

What do you get if the central heating gets stuck on full
in a pet shop ?

Hot dogs !

What did the artist say when he had to choose a pencil ?

2B or not 2B, that is the question !

What game do prisoners like best ?

Cricket - they like to hit and run !

Which vegetable is best at snooker ?

The cue - cumber !

What word is spelled incorrectly in the dictionary ?

'Incorrectly' !

What do you get if you cross a cow
with a monster ?

A horrible mootation !

Which ancient leader invented the salt cellar ?

Sultan pepper !

What is a robot's favourite snack ?

Nuclear fission microchips !

What do you do with a ladder in a hot country ?

Climate !

What do you call a man who looks at the
sky all night long ?

A night watchman !

What animal lives on your head ?

A hare !

Do zombies eat popcorn with their fingers ?

No, they eat the fingers separately !

What was the name of the mechanical writer ?

Robot Louis Stevenson !

Why did the idiot try to spread a goat on his toast ?

Because someone told him it was a butter !

Where should you send a one-legged,
short-sighted man ?

To the hoptician !

What do you get if you cross a bird with a frog ?

Pigeon - toed !

Doctor, are you sure it's my arteries that
are the problem ?

Listen, I'm a doctor, aorta know !

When is a king like a book?

When he has lots of pages!

★

Why did the jelly wobble?

Because it saw the milk shake!

★

Water - a colourless liquid that turns brown
when you put your hands into it!

Why did the idiots stand in an open doorway?

They wanted to play draughts!

Why didn't the idiot's home-made airbag stop him from breaking his nose when he crashed?

He didn't have enough time to blow it up!

Why were the judge and jury on a boat?

Because the prisoner was in the dock!

What sort of food is made from old Chinese boats?

Junk food!

Why did the American Indian chief put smokeless fuel on the fire?

He wanted to send some secret messages!

What do you call a smiling crocodile ?

Snap happy !

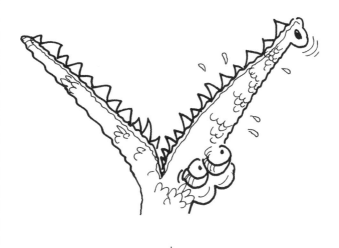

What did the paper say to the pencil ?

You lead me astray !

Why do wolves howl at the moon ?

Because they have such rotten singing voices !

What goes up a drainpipe down but
can't come down a drainpipe up ?

An umbrella !

Did you hear about the man who drove round telling
everyone he was rich and successful, when he
was actually a failure ?

He was a mobile phoney !

Did you hear about the man who drove round telling

How do you know when you come to the
end of a joke book ?

Because there's no more laughing matter !